Bend in Central Oregon

By Raymond R. Hatton

Bend, Oregon, long noted for its attractive site and regional setting, is now one of the most rapidly growing cities in the state. To account for this, one has only to note the unique qualities of this city—its geological setting, its delightful climate, its proximity to the Cascade Range, and its location astride the Deschutes River, where tall pines intermingle with twisted juniper.

Bend in Central Oregon examines the growth of Bend as it has influenced landscape changes. At the turn of this century, it was a small village, with wooden buildings lining dirt streets which vacillated between mud and dust. Irrigation brought water to thirsty Central Oregon acres. Locally produced brick and stone later helped shape the cultural landscape of a growing city. Here, this growth is traced, with original accounts that help the reader relive this period in the city's history.

In 1911, rails enabled settlers to reach Bend more easily and, in 1916, allowed two giant lumber mills to tap the vast pine forests of the Deschutes country. By 1920, Bend had become a bustling city of 5000 people. However, by 1930, alarmists were predicting the end of the lumber city as more and more forests around Bend fell victim to the loggers' onslaughts. Although the population stabilized for a quarter of a century, the city and its nearby High Country were rediscovered in the 1960's when new industries—tourism and recreational land uses—helped revitalize the economy.

Bend in Central Oregon also takes the reader on a tour of various city landmarks. Downtown Bend, located on Mirror Pond, and once the site of the elegant Pilot Butte Inn, is described in print and portrayed with photographs which compare the downtown area as it is today with how it was in earlier years. There are visits to Pilot Butte, a prominent volcano, and Awbrey Heights, site of the campus of Central Oregon Community College.

BEND

In Central Oregon

SCALE OF MILES:

|_____|_____| MILES
      50   100

|_____|_____| KILOMETERS
      100   200

ONE INCH TO 64 MILES.

Bend is located near the center of Oregon, on the Deschutes River, just east of the Cascade Range. The city, by far the largest in Central Oregon, is in Deschutes County, the most rapidly growing county in the state.

BEND

In Central Oregon

By

Raymond R. Hatton

Binford & Mort

Thomas Binford, Publisher

2536 S.E. Eleventh • Portland, Oregon 97202

To Phil F. Brogan, whose half century of
journalism in Bend is reflected in
Bend in Central Oregon

CONTENTS

ACKNOWLEDGMENTS

I wish to express my gratitude to the following—Dr. Bruce Nolf, professor of geology, Central Oregon Community College, Bend; the late Edward A. Groh, Bend; and Larry Chitwood, U.S. Forest Service. All gave of their time for consultation and advice on the geology of the Bend area. Bob Paulson and Tom Oller assisted in the reproduction of many photographs. Peggy Sjogren and Jeff Blevins did excellent work on the maps.

Christine Bohl, Doris Trueax, and Sue Lindbo all contributed to typing the first draft of the manuscript. Special thanks are due Doris Trueax for her fine work in typing the final copy of the manuscript.

Photographs used in the book, other than my own, came from several different sources; each source is identified.

Thanks are expressed to the two publishers who have permitted me to include extracts from their previously published books; each is identified in the text. Mrs. Maurite C. Polhemus, Portland, is thanked for her gracious permission to use excerpts from *Frontier Doctor*. Kathy Bowman, Bend, kindly provided the section on Sawyer State Park.

Several Bend area residents graciously consented to read the completed manuscript. Gratitude is extended to Dr. and Mrs. Robert L. Bristol, Phil F. Brogan, R. Keith Clark, James L. Crowell, Peggy Sawyer, and Dr. Ward Tonsfeldt for their helpful suggestions, corrections, and advice. In addition, the author greatly appreciates the work performed by Thomas Binford, publisher, and Laura Phillips, editor, of Binford & Mort, who helped create the book from the manuscript.

R.R.H.

INTRODUCTION

Bend is one of the most rapidly growing cities in the state of Oregon. Located on the Deschutes River within the shadows of volcanic, snow-capped peaks of the Cascade Range, Bend has an enviable site and a unique geographical setting. In Bend, tall, stately pines merge with the strange, twisted juniper. Beyond the city, to the west, miles of green forests climb until they are halted by rock and ice on the upper slopes of the Cascades. East of Bend, the juniper lands give way to sage and sand of the windswept High Desert. Within a few miles of the city are numerous recreational opportunities, including camping, fishing, hiking, mountain climbing, rockhounding, nordic skiing, and at Mt. Bachelor ski resort, some of the best alpine skiing in the West.

Throughout the city's history, which extends back to the early years of the twentieth century, the people of Bend have capitalized on the area's resources. Early irrigation projects diverted water from the Deschutes River into canals dug and blasted in the lava rock, and watered the arid lands north of the city. Small lumber mills along the river drew on local pine forests for several years before rail lines extended along the canyon of the Deschutes, reaching Bend in 1911. In 1916, two large lumber companies, Shevlin-Hixon and Brooks-Scanlon, started logging and shipping lumber, tapping the vast pine forests south and west of Bend. By the 1920's, Bend had grown into a city of 8000. A slow but steady growth occurred during the next two decades, but by 1950, the city's population had stabilized.

Here, then, was the modest-sized city of 11,500 that I discovered in the summer of 1957. Although my first visit was only a brief one, the impression was favorable—a bustling and friendly community. On the day of my departure—a clear and crisp July morning—I vividly recollect the bright colors of the gardens in Pioneer Park, the elegance of the Pilot Butte Inn on Wall Street, and the panoramic views from the top of Pilot Butte.

During the next few years, I passed through Bend on several occasions. The attractiveness of the city never failed to impress me. My only regret was a lack of time to explore the nearby lakes, forests, Cascade peaks and other volcanic features. In 1965, while attending the University of Oregon, I selected the topic, "The Impact of Tourism in Central Oregon," for my master's thesis. I spent several weeks living in Bend in the summers of 1966 and 1967, doing research in the city and the surrounding area. Since moving to Bend in 1969, I have witnessed the growth that has occurred in Bend in recent years.

This book traces that growth and development. It examines the geographical setting of the city—its geology, invigorating climate, and the importance of the Deschutes River to the Bend people. It describes various parts of the city—the downtown area, and the prominent landmarks, Pilot Butte and Awbrey Heights; and it traces the historical development of the major parks in Bend—Drake Park, Shevlin Park, Pioneer Park and Juniper Park.

In recent years, the economy of the city has become more diversified. The sale and development of recreational land and the growth of tourism, especially since the opening of Mt. Bachelor Ski Resort, have had considerable impact on the local economy and land use. The livability of Bend has been a large factor in making the city attractive to its residents and to visitors. In addition, Bend has become a regional service center for 75,000 Central Oregonians.

There are those in Bend who view with alarm the sudden influx of people. They point out the consequences of rapid growth—overcrowded schools, escalation in land and housing costs, traffic delays, and greater pressure on local recreational facilities. Other people view more positively the growth of Bend, perhaps feeling that the city's economy is healthy. They welcome expanded shopping facilities brought about by greater purchasing power. These people see that a larger population will help encourage expansion of cultural facilities that can be experienced in larger cities.

Whatever the views, Bend has outgrown its small-town image. Planners forecast 45,000 people in the Bend urban area by 1985. It is important that planning for the Bend of tomorrow be done properly today. Such planning must take into consideration the heritage of the city, its cultural landmarks, and its natural beauty—beauty I originally noted in 1957.

BEND

In Central Oregon

Aerial panorama of parts of downtown Bend, Drake Park, the Deschutes River, the West Hills, and, beyond, pumice-mining scars in forest backdoor to Bend. In the background, left to right, are Broken Top, South, Middle and North Sister. (Oregon State Highway photo)

1.

GEOGRAPHICAL SETTING

Bend is one of Oregon's major cities east of the Cascades and among the most scenic in the West. A major north-south route—Highway 97—passes through Bend. The city is also located on Highway 20, linking the Willamette Valley with Eastern Oregon and Southern Idaho. With the increased use of highways in recent times, Bend has become a focal point for thousands of motorists traveling through Central Oregon each year, and tourist business has responded to their highway needs.

No other city of comparable size is within 130 miles of Bend. Thus, as Bend has grown, it has become a regional medical and shopping center, serving over 75,000 Central Oregonians.

In many ways, its geographical setting is unique. The Deschutes River, as it meanders through Bend, adds an aesthetic dimension to the city—and the nearby volcanic peaks provide a scenic background. Nature long ago established natural regions within Central Oregon. To the west of Bend, forested lands climb skyward until trapped by the rock, ice and snow of the Cascades. Forest also covers the rolling topography to the south of Bend and, indeed, the coniferous belt extends unbroken for a hundred miles towards Klamath Falls. The northern fringes of Bend are almost exclusively juniper and sagebrush. To the east, junipers yield to the increasing aridity, and sagebrush and sand mark the High Desert.

In Bend, itself, juniper and pines mix in harmonious fashion. The extensive pine forests have provided the resources for lumber industries which have long been the main economic base for the city, while tourism and the development of recreational resorts have capitalized on the diverse scenic beauty of the High Country to the west of Bend.

The Cascade Skyline

Bend lies right in the shadow of the Cascade Mountains, the volcanic spine of Oregon. Indeed, so prominent and photogenic are the snow-capped Cascades that amateur and professional photographers alike delight in trying to capture the various moods of the mountains. These moods change throughout the day and seasonally.

The Cascade peaks, rising over 10,000 feet in elevation and some 7,000 feet higher than Bend, are lofty enough to intercept the morning rays of the sun several minutes before they flood the high lava plain and drown Bend in sunlight. Given the right atmospheric conditions, the white volcanic peaks to the west of Bend take on a pinkish hue.

Throughout the morning hours, the mountains often glisten and sparkle in the bright sun. Come afternoon, the luster temporarily disappears from the Cascades as the sun "moves" across the southern skies before beginning its "descent" behind the range. Suddenly, as the sun disappears behind the higher peaks, the western skyline again comes alive and into focus. If the atmosphere cooperates, a gorgeous sunset lingers for Central Oregonians to watch or photograph. This sunset, undoubtedly a colorful ritual in Bend country since the birth of the volcanic peaks, was so impressive that it made "news" in *The Bulletin* three quarters of a century ago:

It was cloudy and darkness came early, but the sun got down under the edge of the blanket of clouds and made a flambeau of their lining at 7:30 o'clock. The sharp crest of the Cascade

Range made a jagged floor for the splendid scene. The western side of all objects out of doors was lighted as from a campfire. The somber clouds rolled above; the rushing river below flashed and gurgled; else all was quiet. The flaming sky gradually cooled and the sun slept.[1]

The Cascades are often accurate barometers to weather observers in Bend. As lowering clouds obscure the peaks and gusting winds pick up dust and play havoc with hair styles and hats, the pending storm adds elements of excitement to the atmosphere. No matter what the season, the changing Cascade skyline creates conversation, merits radio reports, and commands newspaper coverage.

Throughout much of the summer, clear skies for days on end prevail in Bend country. A blue sky contrasts markedly against the glacier-clad Three Sisters. Periodically, a gathering thunderstorm adds variety and character to the western horizon as dark cumulo-nimbus clouds, pierced by jagged lightning, shroud the peaks. After a long, dry summer, Bendites get tired of gazing at their soiled peaks. As glaciers recede and become collectors of dust, it seems that the Three Sisters actually diminish in stature.

Bachelor Butte's northern flanks, clearly visible from Bend, become darker as the summer advances. In fact, at times, when U.S. Olympic skiers are reportedly schussing down the perennial glacial bowl near the summit in late summer, there are those who may question if the mountain's ski reputation will withstand the sun's onslaught. By September, curiously enough often around Labor Day, a late summer storm of Pacific origin moves across the Cascades, often bringing with it the "first snow of the season." This snow, light as it may be, gives renewed scenic qualities to the Cascades, which seem to grow again in stature, as clear, dry air replaces the smoke and haze of late summer.

Fall is often a photographer's dream in Bend, with fresh snow on the mountains, a backdrop to a variety of Central Oregon landscapes—alpine meadow, forest-fringed lakes, colorful leaves on deciduous trees, juniper-studded plateaus and green, irrigated pastures. Subsequent fall snows bring out Bend's ski enthusiasts. Despite radio reports of three inches of new snow at Bachelor Butte, I've known college students to drive to Bachelor to check personally on the three inches, as if they absolutely refused to take second-hand information. Such is ski fever in Bend!

Throughout the winter season, fluctuating depths of snow at Bachelor are headline-making stories. However, the Cascade skyline, as seen from Bend, usually changes little except that the snow line in the forest foothills advances and retreats up and down the eastern slopes of the mountains.

By spring, a warming sun begins to melt mountain snow, and Central Oregonians take on new interests in the Cascade landscapes—hiking, fishing, camping, and mountain climbing.

Any time of the year, the Cascade skyline, even though some twenty miles away, adds character to the Bend landscapes. It is hard to imagine Bend without it!

Bend's Volcanic Landscape

Located in volcanic country, Bend lies at a junction where east-sloping lavas from the High Cascades meet lava which spread northwest on the flanks of Newberry Volcano. Indeed, the city and the surrounding areas are characterized by landscapes that reflect different types of volcanic activity. Pilot Butte (elevation 4,138 feet) is a prominent cinder cone, rising 500 feet above the flat lava plain just 2 miles east of downtown Bend. A paved road spirals up the butte, and from the summit a 360-degree panorama of Central Oregon unfolds in an instant.

Awbrey Heights—whose highest point is nearly 100 feet higher than Pilot Butte—is an older and more complex volcano, with multiple vents and many basaltic outcrops. Awbrey Heights, or Awbrey Butte as it is more commonly known, crowds against the Deschutes River and dominates the skyline northwest of downtown Bend. Both Pilot Butte and Awbrey Heights are described in more detail in later chapters. Overturf

Butte (elevation 3,909 feet), located southwest of Bend, is another older volcano that provides good views of parts of Bend and the Cascades.

Where streams have carried eroded material down from the slopes of the High Cascades and Newberry Volcano—such as along the Deschutes River south of Bend, in Bend near Kenwood School, and adjacent to Tumalo Creek near its confluence with the Deschutes River—deposits of sand and gravel are exposed at or near the surface.

Many of the old stream valleys and topographical low spots west of Bend have been filled in by ash flows which were discharged by violent volcanic explosions occurring in the High Country southwest and west of Bend. Many Bend residents and visitors to the area cannot help noticing the extensive white pumice deposits in the lands west of Bend, and the various colored "rimrocks" in Shevlin Park, at Awbrey Meadows north of Central Oregon Community College, and along the Deschutes River near the Brooks-Scanlon Mill.

About 600,000 years ago, volcanic explosions, similar to those which destroyed the town of St. Pierre in the Caribbean in 1902, sent avalanches of volcanic fragments hurtling down canyons toward where Bend is now located. Because of high temperatures, perhaps 1000° Celsius, the exploded fragments were initially in a "plastic" condition. The ash-flow cloud, being extremely dense and highly fluid, since it consisted of gases which had just come out of solution, did not blanket the countryside as explosions of volcanic cinders would do. Rather, the ash flow, kept low by gravity, was concentrated in canyons and low-lying areas. The ash-flow material (commonly called tuff) welded together when it came to rest and, in some instances, when cooled, developed columnar jointing.

Recent studies by Koji Mimura, a Japanese geologist and a recognized expert on volcanic-ash flows, indicates that earlier ash flows in the area west of Bend came from a source near Lookout Mountain and Sitkum Butte (southwest of Bend), and upper (later) deposits may have originated near Broken Top

Volcano.² Geologists generally agree that while such violent volcanic outbursts are now unlikely in the Bend area, Bend and the surrounding areas would be vulnerable to the destruction, should similar activity occur in the Three Sisters country.

The present-day landscapes of the "canyonlands" where the ash flow has hardened are interesting. In places, resulting rock formations have a pinkish or reddish hue, the coloring caused by the sublimation of hematite (iron). Other rimrocks are dark gray or black (as are the east walls of Tumalo Creek in Shevlin Park), or brown to red-brown (as along the Deschutes River at Tumalo State Park). Historically, as will be discussed in the next chapter, the ash-flow material was used in the construction of many early-day buildings in Bend. Even today, black volcanic tuff is cut and transported to Portland as a building stone. Whatever the coloring, the ash-flow deposits have added an aesthetic dimension to the already picturesque pine and juniper lands near Bend.

The large pumice deposits west of Bend cover 30 square miles and, in some places, are as much as 60 feet thick where the flow of hot gases encountered Awbrey Heights and Overturf Butte. Pumice is a light-colored, cellular, almost frothy rock made up of glass-walled bubble casts resulting from the violent expansion of gases in a viscous rhyolite or dacite magma. Pumice differs from the volcanic tuff described above in that the heat of the ash-flow pumice was not as great as that of the tuff and did not weld. In places, there are clearly seen contacts between underlying white pumice deposits and pink, welded ash flow.

The vast pumice deposits near Bend form the basis for important mining and processing industries. Pumice is used for a variety of purposes, including building blocks, soil conditioner, heat and sound insulation, and the polishing of glass, metal, leather, wood, and so forth. In recent years, as much as 380,000 cubic yards of pumice were mined annually in the Bend-Tumalo area—and deposits are expected to last about 50 years. There has been reclamation of some of the recently mined pumice pits,

The Cascades, west of Bend, act as physical barriers to the movements of people and Pacific-born air masses. In this photo, moist air from the Pacific Ocean piles up thick clouds on the windward (western) side of the Three Sisters while Central Oregon basks in sunshine. Mountains in photo, all over 10,000 feet, are, left to right, South Sister, North Sister and Middle Sister, which is partially hidden. (Oregon State Highway photo)

Thick deposits of pumice, laid down by violent volcanic explosions, form the basis of an important mining and manufacturing industry in Bend.

but in other places, deep, white troughs left after the mining ceased have created ready-made garbage dumps, rifle-shooting ranges, and hills on which dirt-bike riders perform. The white, flour-like pumice quickly creates its own clouds when disturbed by man or wind; and during dry, windy spells, clouds of pumice dust fill the otherwise clear air of Bend.

Bend is also at the junction where the High Cascades abut against the Brothers Fault Zone. Pleistocene lava flows have been faulted along northwest trending faults. Although displacements are relatively small, the resulting rimrocks created by the faults—as seen near St. Charles Medical Center and near Fourth Street by Marshall School—add character to Bend's landscapes.

Geological events have certainly played important roles in shaping the landscapes of the Bend area, and in contributing to the diversity of the main topographical features described above. Lava outcrops, pressure ridges, and rimrocks add their own particular aesthetics. In places, homes perched on such ridges or lava outcrops have extensive panoramic views of the Cascade Mountains, and across the juniper lands to the east of Bend.

The volcanic rock in Bend makes construction of utility trenches, house foundations, and city streets expensive undertakings. Blasting of lava rock is time consuming, noisy, and adds to the already high cost of construction. Bend is presently facing the necessity and huge expense (estimated cost is $50 million of which $9 million will come from local sources) of constructing a sewer system. For the greater part of Bend, sewage disposal so far has been accomplished by discharging water wastes into drill holes bored through the volcanic rock.

Many streets dead end at rocky lava tumuli, creating frustration and detours for unwary motorists who are used to the north-south, east-west grid system typical of the West. Curiously enough, maps that depict Bend platted and subdivided show many of these dead-end streets as thoroughfares. Vacant lots are becoming increasingly scarce, and many of these are often, in part, large rockpiles.

Near Bend are some of the most recent volcanic features to be seen within the contiguous United States. The Lava Lands, an area of fresh cinder cones, twisted flows of lava and year-round, ice-cold caves, is situated only ten miles south of Bend. A giant caldera at the summit of Newberry Volcano, with two "Crater Lakes," East and Paulina, is but thirty miles distant.

The diversity of the Bend area landscapes has been recognized by many Bend businessmen. Realtors, restaurant owners, printers, glass dealers, motel operators and others have used words such as "timberline," "alpine," "pine," "Cascades," "desert," "Juniper" and "sun" to name their businesses.

The Deschutes River

The Deschutes River, which originates out of Little Lava Lake east of the Cascades, is a major landscape feature of Central Oregon. In its winding course through the Bend urban area, the river flows in various moods. In general, both upstream and downstream from Bend, it is a turbulent stream, roaring through canyon walls that tower up to 200 feet above the river channel. In places, these walls are comprised of dark, basaltic lava rocks—or rimrocks, as they are locally known. These rimrocks make access to the Deschutes difficult, but the rugged grandeur, and the relative isolation of the Deschutes, only a mile or so from the center of Bend, is one of many geographical factors that make Bend what it is. Only in a couple of places have residential developments blocked public access to the Deschutes along the rimrocks, although other rimrocks are in private hands.

Upstream from Bend, volcanic ash-flow deposits are exposed along the banks of the Deschutes. It was these pinkish-tinted canyon walls which provided rock for the construction of buildings in the early days. Just south of Bend, the Deschutes emerges from its canyon-restricted channel and abruptly changes its somewhat wild mood to one more placid and tranquil. It has created wide, curvaceous bends within the city,

The Deschutes River, upstream and downstream from Bend, flows in a deep canyon. It was logical that the site of Bend, where the Deschutes was forded, was chosen as the location for a settlement. Photo (top) was taken two miles upstream from Brooks-Scanlon mill. Lower photo is north of Pioneer Park where Awbrey Heights (left) abuts the Deschutes.

before taking off in more untamed fashion north of town, where it resumes its rush to the Columbia River.

The site of Bend on the Deschutes River was not selected at random. Where Bend is now located, the Deschutes was easily forded by travelers. And, long ago, Indian trails passed through the area, crossing the Deschutes at fordable places. For many miles upstream and downstream, the river is incised in deep canyons. It is not surprising that man has long used the gentle accessible banks of the Deschutes. Indeed, before Bend was more than a village, a satellite settlement south of Bend was established. Early in the twentieth century, the newspaper *Deschutes Echo* noted:

The place to stop when at Bend is Staats, built in 1886 with lumber from Prineville. Beautifully located on the Deschutes River, it offers fine fishing, it houses a post office (receipts in 1889 averaged 75 cents a month), and is a stage office on the Prineville-Silver Lake route. Board is $5.00 week, meals at 25 cents each and 25 cents feeds the horses overnight. [The Staats house burned down in March, 1929.][3]

In late 1902, John Sisemore constructed a new hotel facing the Deschutes above Bend. The Sisemore log cabin was long a landmark on the meadow next to the river, before its deteriorated state and the demand for using the land for industrial purposes led to its destruction in 1922.

Where the Deschutes makes a wide curve south of Bend, the landscape scene for the most part is now an industrial one. Brooks-Scanlon's vast lumber operations line the eastern banks of the stream. Three tall, unused stacks, and a maze of buildings and pipes are prominent features of the mill. Farther back from the river, a particle board plant—under the ownership of Willamette Industries—also contributes to the industrial setting. Although other industries are scattered throughout the zoned industrial land, it is the sights and the not unpleasant wood smells that create a general feeling that lumber and wood products are a major part of the Bend area's economy.

Sisemore place along the Deschutes River, about 1914. This is near the site of the present Brooks-Scanlon Mill. (Phil F. Brogan photo)

Aerial view of Brooks-Scanlon mill and Deschutes River (foreground) and (beyond) the city of Bend. Industrial site of disused Shevlin-Hixon mill is to west of the Deschutes. Brooks-Scanlon employs about 900 workers, has an annual payroll of over $12 million. Brooks-Scanlon, as a matter of corporate policy, sets aside 2% of its pretax income for philanthropic purposes to help improve the quality of life in communities in which the company operates. (Delano Photographics, Portland, and Brooks-Scanlon Corp., Bend)

While the hustle and bustle of the day's activities are conspicuous parts of the landscape in the Brooks-Scanlon - Willamette Industries area, to the west of the Deschutes, the almost ghostly remains of the Shevlin-Hixon plant, sold to Brooks-Scanlon in the early 1950's, must bring nostalgia to former employees. Parts of the Shevlin-Hixon property, adjacent to the west bank of the Deschutes, lie barren, except for rusting metal, blocks of concrete, foundations, and scattered, weatherworn pieces of lumber. Some of the larger mill structures still stand. Indeed, industrial activity hums from the inside of their rather dilapidated structures. A wooden trestle, which for years carried rail freight from Shevlin-Hixon across the Deschutes River, is still part of the contemporary landscape. However, a modern concrete bridge connects the two sides of the Deschutes for road traffic.

Before the river lazily drifts past Drake and Harmon Parks, it slices through older residential areas and borders Columbia Park. The latter is a small community park located on flat land separated from the river by giant blocks of volcanic tuff. A narrow footbridge links Columbia Park with the residential areas on the east bank of the Deschutes.

Land adjacent to any river in an urban area is much in demand, and high priced. Next to Pioneer Park in Bend, the Bend Riverside Motel and Condominium Apartments flank the Deschutes, effectively blocking public access along the eastern bank of the stream. One mile downstream, The Riverhouse— a modernly constructed motel and restaurant complex designed to blend naturally into the landscape—is built so close to the Deschutes that motel guests and restaurant diners sleep and eat in a near-total water environment. Between the two motel complexes is a little-known but scenic tract of private land. Here, canyon walls, small, woody meadows and the turbulent river meet.

Diversion dams near the north entrance to Bend have created a replica of the Mirror Pond to be found upstream at Drake Park. The dark water of the river forms an aquatic backyard for the few fortunate residents whose homes border the Deschutes at this point.

During the irrigation season, much of the water from the Deschutes River is diverted into the North Unit and Central Oregon Irrigation Canal systems, leaving but a very weak ghost of a river to trickle past the Riverhouse Restaurant and Motel. Robert W. Sawyer Park, a small but scenic and relatively untamed state park, named after the former *Bulletin* publisher, straddles the Deschutes just downstream from The Riverhouse. The character and the setting of the park landscape is well described by Kathy Bowman of Bend:

A thumbnail flat of green and high, dark bluffs against a reedy edge of the Deschutes River is Sawyer State Park. A sturdy plank footbridge leads from the narrow crescent of green to an undeveloped hillside of junipers on the opposite side. The water is mostly quiet here. It moves slowly among the cattails and water-smoothed angular stones. Only under the center of the footbridge does it flow swiftly between smooth, potholed basalt rocks. In the green part of the park, a neat asphalt trail curves down from a hedge, screening the little parking lot.

The park is a cozy space. Low junipers hung with mistletoe obscure the roadway and the mobile homes from the view of the park user. At one end of the park is a small, dark bluff or low cliff. The top, ascended by an easier route from the back side, is covered with many little flowering plants and shrubs among the basalt rocks. The small climb gives the hiker a view of the park, the river, and the undisturbed junipers across the river. A feeling of natural greenness, far from the comings and goings of commerce on nearly Highway 97, is possible here. Spaces of green and water and sun give people a chance to rest and forget momentarily their human worries.[4]

Unquestionably, part of the attraction of Bend is having a host of secluded places only a mile or so from the city. Sawyer State Park is but one example.

North of Sawyer State Park, the Deschutes bends around massive Awbrey Heights, a large, ancient, shield volcano. For

Part of the Shevlin-Hixon mill which started operations in 1916, and closed down in 1950. Feasibility studies on the mill buildings will determine if the site and structures could be remodeled and used as a cultural arts center.

Sawyer State Park, north of Bend. Here, the Deschutes has been reduced to a small stream following diversion of water for irrigation.

Diversion dam on Deschutes River north of Bend serves two irrigation canals. Second "Mirror Pond" provides scenic backyard for residences.

What little water is left in the Deschutes, after the diversion for irrigation north of Bend, flows past the "back doors" to the Bend Riverhouse, Motel and Restaurant.

several miles, the river roars between towering canyon walls, some of which now provide abrupt property boundaries to homesites and homes that perch on the rimrock. It is in this rather violent mood that the Deschutes exits from the Bend area.

Bend has only one natural surface stream, the Deschutes River. However, excavations and drilling through lava rock have revealed the presence of an underground "Lost River" and "Pleistocene Mirror Pond." In 1939, sediments of an ancient river were found under 18 feet of basalt while excavations for the Third Street underpass were in progress. Indeed, further test drilling at the site revealed something of the complex geology on which the city is situated. Under the basalt were 14 feet of water-deposited sediment from glaciers, 44 feet of volcanic ash from a mountain explosion, and 19 feet of heavy grey pumice, then fissure lava.

In 1947, drilling on the west side of Bend tapped a subterranean stream. *The Bulletin*, in editorializing the discovery, conjectured on the geological relationships with the Deschutes, and called for further study of the "Lost River":

Over a period of years there have been reports of a "subterranean river" in Bend—a stream that flows through lightless lava crevasses and tumbles over Stygian ledges. This rumored river of the dark caverns was again tapped this week, this time when a test hole was being drilled on Harmon playfield for the proposed municipal swimming tank. Diagonally across the street, on the Kenwood school grounds, the "river" was tapped in pre-war days. The subterranean stream was also found in other drilling work, in westside Bend.

Reports of the lava-cavern stream are fascinating. Definitely, there is a stream coursing through the old lavas, and its presence and the fact that it is being used to carry away sewage pose some questions. Is it a part of the Deschutes flow, escaping into underground fissures? If it is a stream separate from the Deschutes, can the subterranean flow be pumped to the surface to augment the supply of irrigation water? Does the flow, with its sewage, go back into the Deschutes channel at some point downstream? Some answers can be attempted. Dyes or radio-active materials can be placed in the flowing water, for downstream test. Purity tests of the water can be made, and these are planned by the city. If the flow is uncontaminated, this will be proof that it is not carrying sewage from some higher point in its course.

The "lost river" of westside Bend is not a silently flowing stream. It is noisy, and the sound of the flowing water can be heard, once a drill breaks through into lava crevasses, at a depth of 162 feet on the Harmon grounds. The sound is not of a gently flowing stream. It is the roar of an underground cataract. This has led to the conclusion that the water is falling into the crevasses from a higher level, probably around the 70-foot level. . . .

Two holes were drilled on Harmon field in the quest for an underground drainage cavern, and it was the first hole, bored to a depth of 270 feet, that provided a significant development. At the 160-foot level, a flow of semiartesian water was struck. This surged up the 6-inch hole to within a few feet of the top. Here was a possible new supply of irrigation water, apparently independent of the Deschutes river because of its deep source. Drilling was continued in the hunt for the proposed swimming pool drainage and the semiartesian water was lost at the 170-foot level. It is too bad a pumping test could not be made. Water is valuable in Central Oregon these days. The North unit is paying about $10,000,000 for its flow.

Bend's "subterranean river" bears further study. The water, in its race through rocky caverns, may have value other than a carrier of sewage.[5]

According to Phil F. Brogan, Bend, who wrote this editorial, no study of the underground water has been undertaken.

Weather and Climate

Important in any landscape scene are the conditions of the atmosphere. The quality of the air in Bend has long attracted people, including many who had previously suffered from tuberculosis. Bright sunlight, shade, seasonal changes in vegetation, cloud formations, and effects of snow are just some of the atmosphere-related phenomena that influences the physical environment in Bend. In 1918, W.D. Cheney wrote:

I can only leave to the imagination the long twilights at Bend, with the sunset lingering for two hours behind the Cascade Range. I have not the skill to convey to you the beauty of this place or its charm. The climate and its effects on the mind and body are equally indescribable.[6]

Years before Cheney's glowing description, *The Bulletin*, in mid-1903, reported on the weather and its relationships with the small but growing village of Bend:

If anyone knows of a more delightful climate than Bend, we should like to have it pointed out. Look at the weather report for June, published elsewhere in this paper—a mean maximum of 74.1 and a mean minimum of 50.1 degrees, with rain enough to soak the dust in six days. The extremes of temperature were 26 and 92. With a clean, bracing atmosphere, the best water in the world from a brimming river that is perpetually hurrying and carrying to the sea and never becomes unruly, the shade of the whispering pines and junipers, flowers and birds to make all the day gay, Bend can't be beaten as a pleasant and beautiful abiding place. Of course, we miss the opera, the clanging trolly car, the fire brigade, the patrol wagon and the street faker.[7]

More recently recorded comments (in response to an informal survey by the author) follow. These were answers to the question, "What do you like about Bend and Central Oregon?"

"High, dry, sunny and cheerful."
"The sunshine, clear air and beautiful blue sky."
"The dry climate, scent of juniper and sage after rain."
"Warm summers, cold winters with snowfall."
"Seeing the stars at night, taking a deep breath without coughing because of pollution."

Many responses, not surprisingly, were repetitious. It is not appropriate here to give a full detailed analysis of Bend's weather and climate, but rather to summarize and explain when and how meteorological conditions influence perceptions of the landscape.[8] Bend has a dry, continental climate, lying, as it does, east of the Cascades. Summer days are warm [usually in the 70-90° F (21-32° C) range], but because of the clear, dry air at 3,600-feet elevation, rapid loss of heat by radiational cooling results in cool nights. It is usual in summer for minimum temperatures to be around 40° F (4.4° C) but it is not uncommon for the mercury to lower slightly above or below freezing even in July or August. Heavenly bodies stand out in unbelievable clarity in the desert-like air at night.

The deep blue skies mentioned by so many visitors to Bend are due to the purity of the atmosphere, with its absence of air pollution and a minimum of water vapor. Atmospheric gas molecules are much smaller than the wavelengths of visible light from the sun. Therefore, on clear days, the shorter wavelengths of the blue and violet colors are scattered more than the red and yellow colors from the incoming beam of "white" sunshine. Thus, the sky appears a blue color. However, when there are cloud droplets, haze, fog or pollutants—which have diameters as large as or larger than the wavelengths of sunlight and which do not show a preference for scattering any particular wavelengths—all are scattered equally. Thus when the atmosphere is hazy or cloudy or polluted, the sky appears white. It is important for atmospheric pollutants be controlled, if Bend is to maintain its blue skies.

It is of little wonder that early residents of Bend, as noted above, saw fit to comment on an agreeably pleasant June. The attractive summer climate certainly contributes to the large-scale and micro-scale perceptions of the landscapes. The sharpness and crispness of the early mornings brings out, with remarkable clarity, distant peaks of the Cascade Range.

It is quite common to stand on Pilot Butte and see Mt. Hood rising above the distant hills, beyond the Deschutes Plateau nearly 100 miles to the north. And it is not unusual to see the high, glacial-clad dome of 12,000-foot Mt. Adams in

Tall Ponderosa pines cast long shadows across snow-covered Drake Park. Wooden bridge (left) is for pedestrians or bicyclists only. Many homes on West Hills (background) have commanding views over the city of Bend.

Snow drapes trees and bushes around Mirror Pond, providing sufficient depth for cross-country skiers in Drake Park.

Wall Street buried by nearly 4 feet of snow in December, 1919. View is looking north. Pilot Butte Inn is in (left) background. (Jim Arbow photo)

The "Big" snow and freeze, December 1919. Temperatures plunged to -25°F following 47 inches of snow being dumped on the city in two days. (Jim Arbow photo)

Washington State, 125 miles distant. The Three Sisters and Bachelor Butte, 20 miles to the west, seem so close in the morning air that they almost look within hiking distance.

On a microscale, especially after a light rain or morning dew, the Bend air, indeed that of much of Central Oregon, is perfumed by the fragrant scent from sage, juniper and pine, which intermingle. Blue skies contrast markedly with the deep green foliage and the cinnamon-colored trunks of ponderosa pine. Early in the morning, the warming rays of the sun are welcomed as they temper the coolness characteristic of shady areas. By mid-afternoon, the same shade offers sought-after relief from a much more ferocious sun.

Although many Bend residents opt for natural landscaping, with pine, juniper, and sagebrush, there are enough people with green thumbs who conscientiously work to add color to their gardens. Throughout Bend, flower gardens literally sparkle in the clear, dry air, their bright colors brought out by watering every other day—and by their marked contrast to the natural green and brown landscapes.

Spring landscapes in Bend often alternately reflect the successful attempts of nature to make the transition to summer, and the determined efforts of winter to cover everything with a light snowfall. Nature, wisely, is hesitant to yield prematurely to summer, patiently biding its time to come out of winter hibernation. Bend residents, not by choice, must endure spring, a rather drab season as far as landscape scenes go. Although Bend is better noted for its coniferous trees, a surprising number of deciduous trees are spread throughout the city. These show up best in the fall as cold night-time temperatures contribute to the changing colors. The atmosphere, at times hazy with the burning of fields in Jefferson County to the north, or slash in the nearby forests, becomes more subdued. Even so, fall in Bend is a favorite season for many residents and tourists, with warm days followed by crisp nights.

Snow always adds a special effect to the landscape, especially when blue skies follow the end of a storm. Snow sparkles in the bright sunlight, contrasting against the blue sky and the green foliages of the juniper and ponderosa pine. On a microscale, winter landscape scenes that are characteristic of the Bend area are to be seen when dark basalt rocks and sagebrush are blanketed by snow. Meanwhile, in town, cultural features take on a festive appearance, especially if coinciding with the Christmas season. There are decorations and lights—and Bend's Parks and Recreation District's horse-drawn sleigh is used to carry children and adults around the downtown streets. Most homes in Bend feature fireplaces, which (even if not energy efficient) continue to add psychological warmth and comfort to families any time of the year.

2.

GROWTH OF BEND

The City is Named

The name of the city did not come about in an easy way. Indeed, it is not simple to keep track of all the different names that have been appended to the city astride the Deschutes River. There is on record, for example, mention of at least two Indian names for the geographical location where Bend later was to take shape. In 1927, Lewis A. McArthur, author of *Oregon Geographic Names*, was informed by Captain O.C. Applegate of Klamath Falls that the Warm Springs Indian name for the ford, where the city of Bend is now situated, was Wychick. However, no translation of the word was given.[9]

A brief article in *The Bulletin* stated that before the coming of the white man, the Deschutes Valley was called Quelah—The Beautiful Valley, and the place where Bend now stands was known to the Indians as Widgi Creek.[10]

Perhaps just as important as the fact that Indian names were applied to the site of Bend is the fact that the city is located in what, at one time, was Indian country, and Indian artifacts are part of the archaeology of the Bend area, as will be noted later.

The name of Bend is an abbreviation of one of the original names for the settlement. Farewell Bend was a place on the Deschutes River where travelers on the pioneer stage road had

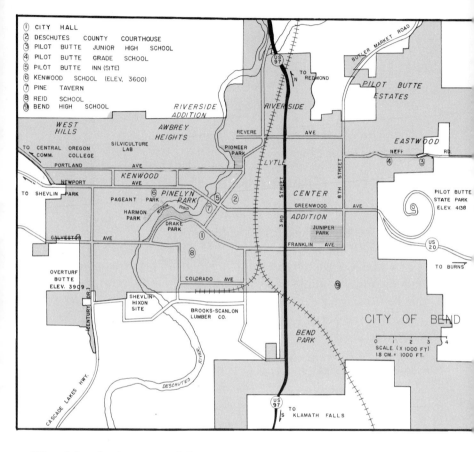

City of Bend, showing subdivisions mentioned in this chapter along with other major geographical features discussed in the book.

their last view of the river. The name was shortened by postal authorities to "Bend" but later, in 1903, for a short time, the city was known as "Deschutes." Commenting on the short-lived name change, the *Deschutes Echo*, wrote:

Bend is dead. The Post Office on the Deschutes River which has borne that cramped up name for so many years passed quietly into the sleep that knows no awakening. The man who sat on the bank of the river thirty years ago and after enduring a severe spasm gave the place the hysterical name of Bend has not been heard from.

Deschutes! That sounds better, looks better, writes better and in fact makes everyone who has been compelled to endure the opprobrium attached to the name of Bend, feel better. Consequently everyone is satisfied. It is no longer Bend, Broke or Busted but plain and rhythmical Deschutes. A petition circulated several weeks ago indicated that residents feel that Deschutes is more distinctive of the town location, a town located on the Deschutes River in the Deschutes Valley and in that part of Crook County known as the Deschutes Country.[11]

The name change from "Bend" to "Deschutes" lasted only from January, 1903, to March, 1904, before the Post Office reversed the name back to "Bend." Other names which have unsuccessfully applied to Bend include "Pilot Butte" and "Staats," the old stage office located just south of Bend.

Others echoed the sentiment that the name "Bend" was not particularly inspiring. In 1910, *The Bulletin* reported that it was "a handicap for a town destined to be one of the great cities in the region," and came up with two alternatives. One suggestion was "Lenark," derived from Lewis and Clark. The alternative was "Oreopolis," adding the word "opolis" (city) to the first part of the name of the state.[12]

As already stated, Bend was at one time part of Indian country. Throughout Central Oregon, countless discoveries of Indian artifacts have been revealed. Indian camps have been located along the flanks of lava flows, in caves, at stream crossings and other watering places, and in meadows. Indians did not shun the site of Bend, and research through old *Bulletins* reveals several articles on the location and the nature of such finds. These discoveries were well summarized in this editorial of April 4, 1936:

There is every indication that the present site of Bend, on an easily accessible portion of river that through most of its long gorge rushes through rugged canyons, for ages was used by Indians as a camping ground. Within the past 20 years, three large caches of arrow and spear points, all made of black obsidian, were found within the city limits of Bend. Some of these points were of the type used by aborigines in hunting buffaloes and are probably relics of that age when great herds of bison ranged over Central Oregon.

Street grading work in Bend, especially on that portion of Drake road near the Drake park footbridge, frequently brings to light bits of chipped flint and parts of arrowheads. Children excavating on vacant lots immediately east of the Kenwood school have found chipped stones several feet under ground.

But the most important finds made in Bend have been the result of basement excavation work. Old files of *The Bulletin* hold stories of the discovery of stone knives even at depths of eight feet, in apparently undisturbed soil. There is every reason to believe that some of the artifacts unearthed in Bend were of the same crude and ancient workmanship as those removed from the Wickiup Dam excavation, but the value to science of the Bend relics was not recognized.

To John Issackson, one of the reclamation service workmen who found the stone knives of the "Deschutes man," should be given full credit for directing scientific attention to the Wickiup relics. Like a true scientist, he carefully noted the level at which the knives were found, observed the undisturbed condition of the soil, then reported his discovery.

Bend Awaits the Railroad

The early history of the Bend Country has been vividly described by Phil Brogan in his book, *East of the Cascades*. This section, on Bend's growth since the start of the twentieth

A.M. Drake residence and lawn, 1910. *The Bulletin*, April 15, 1904, reported "A.M. Drake has devoted a great deal of attention to the improvement of the 3-1/2 acre lot in which his residence is located. It has been plowed, harrowed, rolled and scraped to perfect smoothness, and given sufficient slope for convenient irrigation. It will be converted into a model lawn." (Claude H. Kelley photo)

Early twentieth-century irrigation flume under construction south of Bend. Because of the arid climate in Central Oregon, irrigation has been essential for growth of crops and alfalfa. Construction of irrigation flumes and canals stimulated employment and population in Bend as well as creating the need for lumber. (Oregon Historical Society photo)

Wall Street looking South in 1904. The post office in the foreground was located where Equitable Savings & Loan is now. Note the wooden sidewalks and unpaved street. (Frances Barry photo)

Wall Street in 1906. The post-office building has been enlarged and several new buildings constructed. (Frances Barry photo)

century, focuses on the changing landscapes of the community. In the early years of its existence, Bend was nothing more than a frontier village, although the Deschutes River, where Bend is located, was visited by trappers, explorers, migrants and stockmen. Ranchers settled on grassy meadows along the upper Deschutes in Bend country during the last quarter of the nineteenth century.

It was not until 1900 that Alexander M. Drake, a midwestern businessman looking for new opportunities in the West, settled along the Deschutes and built the log cabin shown in the photograph on page 29. However, Charles Hutchinson was the first land developer in Bend to use irrigation water from the Deschutes River. In need of capital, Hutchinson met Drake at Spokane and lured him to Bend, but Drake decided to "strike out on his own." Under Drake's direction, land was surveyed and platted, and Drake's Pilot Butte Development Company delivered water to the arid lands near Bend.

The early landscape changes in Bend were noted by *The Deschutes Echo*, 1902:

The little sagebrush flat called Bend upon which two years ago stood a single log cabin and a post office, has sprung suddenly into life—a living, struggling community reaching forth for prestige, support and investment to develop the wealth of resources lying adjacent to its doors. The sagebrush no longer obscures the post office but has given way to broad fields of rye, clearings, flowered fields, fences, barns and other indications of growth.

The lava ridges, which a few months ago laughed in derision at the mere suggestion of buildings, have fallen in line—succumbed to the energy of the community which stops not at piles of rocks, but masters their crudeness and uses them for building supports and foundations.

For half a mile on either side of the post office at Bend, the Deschutes River is dotted with houses, more are being built, two hotels week after week are crowded to their fullest capacity and a third is now under course of construction. Even at that, Bend is a canvas town and the dimensions at that side

Wall Street in 1962, looking south from approximately the same place as the 1904 and 1906 photos. Wall Street was still two-way and was on the main north-south highway through Central Oregon.

Looking south on Wall Street, 1978, from the same location as 1904 photo. The street, at this point, is now one way, and because of the population increase, receives considerably more traffic.

of the place are likely to be increased before another summer
has come. It is simply a case of live under eight ounces of
ducking or stay out of doors. Houses are not to be had and
lumber is now at a premium.

M.J. Scanlon, the millionaire lumberman from Minnesota,
looked the field over pretty thoroughly while here a few weeks
ago. "Give me the power of the magnificent river back in Minnesota, and I will make it worth $500,000 to myself in six
months time."[13]

It is significant to note that the above report was written in
December, a month when tent living was indicative of the
pioneer spirit of the people moving to Bend.

We can turn the calendar back and visit Bend and its regional
setting as Dr. Urling C. Coe, Bend's first doctor, described it in
1905:

Two little saw mills, one at the upper end of town run by
steam and one below town run by water power from the river,
were going full blast to turn out lumber for the building
operations, and a brickyard was soon to be opened. There were
eight saloons with open gambling and a lusty red light district
consisting of several small shacks on the river bank in the lower
end of town. There was hurry and bustle on all sides with a
tang of romance and excitement in the air. The hotel was over-
flowing with new guests continually arriving, and the stores,
saloons, and streets were full of busy, excited people.

Freighters, stockmen, buckaroos, sheep herders, timber
cruisers, gamblers, and transients of all kinds who had been
attracted to the town by the boom, thronged the bars or played
at the gambling games, and the stores were doing a rushing
business. The stores remained open in the evenings and the
saloons stayed open all night and all day Sunday, and many of
the laborers from the construction camps spent the weekends in
town, drinking, gambling, carousing, or fighting.

Every stage that came the hundred miles from the end of the
railroad was loaded with new settlers. Big freight wagons,
usually with a trailer or two hooked on behind and drawn by
ten to sixteen horses, brought tons of freight of all kinds into

town and went back to the railroad loaded with hides, pelts, and wool from the big stock ranches in the interior.

In addition to the railroad freight charges, merchants had to pay three cents a pound and sometimes more to have their merchandise hauled in from the end of the railroad. That made it very costly, but everyone seemed to have plenty of money and spent it freely. Exciting rumors heard on all sides were to the effect that the Hill and Harriman Lines would soon start building railroads into Bend to tap the timber of the largest virgin pine forest in the United States. Real estate men and timber locators were doing a brisk business, while the prices of city property, irrigated and farm lands, and timber were soaring steadily upward.

Stretching away for hundreds of miles to the east and southeast from the town was a vast expanse of semi-arid, rolling plateau country, covered with sage brush, bunch grass, and occasional small patches of scrubby juniper trees, and dotted here and there with large stock ranches. This vast un-fenced area constituted the great stock ranges of eastern Oregon, southern Idaho, northern Nevada, and northeastern California. It was the largest area in the United States without a railroad, and the last frontier of the thrilling and romantic Old West. It was the home of the jack rabbit, the coyote, the badger, the bobcat, the sagehen, the big mule deer and the fleet and graceful prong-horned antelope. Here, also, thousands upon thousands of wild range horses, cattle and sheep grazed on the open range all year around.

In the forest country across the river, big game of all kinds was plentiful, and the clear mountain lakes and sparkling streams swarmed with many varieties of gamey trout.[14]*

With rumors that Bend was destined to be the terminus of the Columbia Southern Railroad, coupled with visions of developing water power from the Deschutes, and the start of development of irrigation across the desert near Bend, real estate in the city became much in demand. Late in 1902, lots 40 x 110 feet were priced from $40 to $60 each. Two years later, land near Bend was advertised for $2.50 an acre, but city lots in

*Urling C. Coe, *Frontier Doctor.* Copyright 1940 by Macmillan Publishing Co., New York.

One of several waterwheels used to pump water from Deschutes for houses in Bend, about 1904. (Deschutes County Library photo)

Freighters in Wall Street, Bend, about 1910, a time when most of the buildings were constructed of wood. View is looking south. (Deschutes County Library photo)

The Shaniko-Bend stage coach, 1910. Teams of horses changed every 20 miles. It took 12 hours to cover the 100-mile journey. (Claude H. Kelley photo)

Ten-horse outfit pulling 3 wagons (laden with pipes) in Bend early in the twentieth century. Driver on horse controlled the lead horse with a feed line. Signals along the line "instructed" the lead horse which directions to take. (Deschutes County Library photo)

the commercial section commanded soaring prices. A lot on the north corner of Bond and Minnesota, the site of a saloon, sold for $450.

North of Bend, adjacent to the Deschutes River, the Steidl-Reed lumber mill, built at a cost of $12,800, had started operations. Lumber from this mill and another mill south of town contributed to the community's rapid growth. Even so, Bend seemingly was surrounded by an untamed world, but with nature and "civilization" beginning to clash. Bears and cougars were frequently reported seen in the vicinity. In 1904, it was reported that a "three-year-old black bear swam the Deschutes River just below Bend and struck out for a rendezvous on the eastern desert. That was the bear's fatal error. He didn't know of Bend's rapid growth. The bear was shot after crossing the river."

Coe writes of his early days (1905) in Bend:

When I first came to town, I started a diary in which I planned to record the important events of my first year of practice. I was soon much too busy to keep it up. But I noted my arrival in Bend on the tenth. A black bear visited town by swimming the Deschutes River on the thirteenth. Two huge mountain lions visited town, one on the twelfth, the other on the fifteenth. On the sixteenth a rancher rode in with a lion tied on the back of his saddle. It was only a moderately sized lion, but measured seven feet from nose to tail.[15] *

Bend's rapid growth now no longer threatens the tracks of bears, although as recently as 1958, a 200-pound black bear was treed and killed in the yard of a residence on Galveston Avenue. Today, suburbanization is rapidly encroaching on the winter grazing lands for deer.

The changing urban landscape in Bend, from its beginning at the turn of the century to 1906, was reported in *The Bulletin* by a visitor from Portland. He noted that in 1902, on his last visit to Bend, there were only a half dozen buldings, apart from Mr. Drake's residence and stables, a log school house, and the Pilot

*Urling C. Coe, *Frontier Doctor*. Copyright 1940 by Macmillan Publishing Co., New York.

Land promotion in Bend in 1913. At that time, Bend was part of Crook County. Note the use of volcanic tuff for building stone. This photo was taken on the east side of Bond Street. (Phil F. Brogan photo)

Scene east of Pilot Butte (right background) about 1904. Notice the absence of trees in this photo. While Ponderosa pine is widespread west of Pilot Butte, juniper trees are typical east of the butte. Land shown in the photo is now being developed. (Deschutes County Library photo)

Butte Inn. This was the original Pilot Butte Inn, predating the famous Hotel opened in 1917. He added:

Now you have a business center with many of the features of a city. For example, your hotels are first class: good food, good sleeping accommodations, good service. You are building a school house that compares favorably with similar structures in towns three times the size of Bend. [16]

Transportation into Bend from anywhere was a difficult and often unpleasant journey until the railroad arrived in 1910. The first auto stage (a 55 H.P. auto with solid rubber tires) between Shaniko and Bend started in April, 1905. The arrival scene and details of the journey were reported in the local press:

The auto arrived in town at 5:30 p.m. The car pulled up at the Pilot Butte Inn and the passengers with landlord Smith then went with Hugh O'Kane to remove dust—from their throats.

The auto had left Shaniko pulling half a tone of baggage and made a leisurely journey. After a rough trip down Cow Canyon, it stopped in Madras two days. At Culver, Sunday School was dismissed while the whole school took a ride in the auto. The running time from Madras to Bend was at 10 mph with a one-hour stop at Forest. [17]

But the real transportation news (or rumors) was the completion of the promised railroad. So great was the rivalry between Bend and Prineville for the railroad terminal in Central Oregon, that a Prineville *Journal* observer noted that *The Bulletin* was building the railroad (again). *The Bulletin* replied, "Now will the *Journal* tell us what it is doing to build up the country."

"Building up the country" certainly must have been the motto of the day. Boosterism and promotion of the area were much in evidence when one researches the newspapers of those early years in Bend. As the railroad construction approached Bend, real estate became more and more in demand. One realtor was reported selling 50 lots in Deschutes Addition in ten days at prices ranging from $125 to $175. Business lots had increased in value to $1000. However, within three miles of Bend, 160 acres of land could be purchased for a $350 total price.

Promotion of land in and near Bend took place on a large scale throughout the Pacific Northwest, particularly in the Seattle area. The Bend Park Company, in compiling *The Bend Book* (1911), reported in glowing terms the bright future of Bend country and the interest being shown in the area:

In one day, on the trail from the railroad to Bend, the writer passed sixty-four wagons. . . . Each of these was said to carry from 3000 to 4000 pounds of freight. . . .[18]

From the top of Pilot Butte, and before us, beside a river, in the midst of a natural park, with snow-capped mountains shining in almost constant sunlight, with air like wine, three thousand six hundred feet above the sea, is Bend. Behind and on both sides of us, the irrigated farms of Wenatchee. Surrounding them, the wheat lands of Minnesota. Before us, the pine lands of Michigan and the power of Niagara. On all sides of us, the scenery of Switzerland.

In the center of this setting, a town, having the altitude of Colorado, the cool summers of Seattle, and a winter climate unlike any other in the world—almost snowless, with clear cold nights and sunny days too warm for furs. Just think of being able to say these things truthfully about any town. It seems as if we were about to enter an immense city instead of a village of six hundred people.[19]

Favorable news of Bend country, its growth and its promise for the future was spread back East. A letter to *The Bulletin* in 1909 stated:

We people back East are hearing a great deal of Central Oregon, particularly the Deschutes region, and reports have been so favorable that many people with whom I am acquainted are planning to become permanent residents of Crook County this coming year. Many of them have sold their wheat farms and are arranging to come early in the spring, along with the rest of the tide of new settlers, which will spring

Construction of the dam and irrigation diversion canal on Deschutes River north of Bend about 1912. Area in the background is where First Street is now located. (Deschutes County Library photo)

Sawmill south of Bend near present-day location of Columbia Park. This mill, which burned down in 1915, lost 5 million board-feet of sawed lumber expected to be used for the two new mills then being built in Bend. Lumber for Shevlin-Hixon and Brooks-Scanlon had to be shipped in to complete the mills. (Deschutes County Library photo)

Bend High football team en route home from playing Crook County High School, Thanksgiving Day, 1910. The 36-mile journey took all day with a stop at Powell Butte for refreshments. The entire team of 13 players and coach and driver, plus equipment, crowded the stage. Crook County was the victor. The team returned to Bend the third day. (Claude H. Kelley photo)

Bend High vs. Crook County High. Game was played at Troy Field on Railroad Day, October 6, 1911, part of a two-day celebration. Crook County won 23-0. (Claude H. Kelley photo)

up in a hundred different sections of the East in 1910 and head
for the Deschutes.

I believe the Deschutes Valley and Bend are the two best
advertised districts on the Pacific Slope today, outside of
California, which, of course, has been in the hands of publicity
bureaus for a great many years. But the immigration into the
Deschutes Valley, next year, will make up for lost time if the interest taken in the region back East and the present plans of
many to come here count for anything.[20]

Curiously enough, one of the attractions of Bend and of
Central Oregon in 1910—as it still is today—was the attempt to
flee the "big city" and return to the country. A Chicago trades-
man, in 1910, stated:

. . .there is a great tendency among the people in my class in
Chicago toward the soil and many have set their hearts on
coming to Oregon. I, along with many more, am getting tired of
this humdrum life, and long for the quiet of the country. There
is a longing for the freedom of the soil—a harking back to the
joys of childhood days on the farm.
I attended the land show here at the Coliseum in November
and will say that Oregon had one of the best exhibits there.
After the show everyone had a notion that they were to become
farmers. Living expenses in Chicago are getting to be so high
that even the most common of food is getting to be a luxury and
rents are going up all the time, so that a man making a small
salary has to be a genius to make both ends meet. Hence the
tendency toward the farm, and the desire to "Go West."[21]

Around 1910, inter-regional rivalry among cities and areas for
prospective migrants was common. Goaded on by local patriotic
newspapers, mud slinging—or "knocking" as it was then
termed—was going on continually. For example, *The Bulletin*
reported receiving a letter from an influential Eastern
gentleman who was interested in Bend but was a little put off
by reports of the climate of the Bend country. The letter states:

One of the things that I am up against is the statement of
some land parties in the Willamette Valley that the Deschutes

Bend's first schoolhouse, later used by *The Bulletin* and the Boy Scouts before being abandoned in 1910. This land later became part of Drake Park. (Deschutes County Library photo)

Valley is high plateau lands, running from four to six thousand feet in altitude and extremely windy with a bad climate. Now you can give me something absolutely correct on this particular subject, and will you do it as soon as possible, and greatly oblige.[22]

The Bulletin, evidently concerned by this misrepresentation of Central Oregon, replied:

One district's "knocking" of another is so prevalent as scarcely to merit attention, yet for the benefit to the Eastern inquirer and the misrepresenting webfooter, these statements may service a purpose. The Deschutes Valley varies in altitude from one to 5,000 feet, the latter figure really including no territory which properly can be reckoned part of the valley. Most emphatically Central Oregon is not a windy country; with the exception of a few spring wind storms it is notably free from this annoyment. Equally emphatically we state—and challenge contradiction—that no climate in the west surpasses that of the Bend Country.

Bend School Building, 1914, used by grades 1-12. High School occupied the top floor. All students lived within walking distance to school, which was located near land now used by courthouse annex. Built at a cost of $6,500, according to *The Bulletin* (Sept. 14, 1906) it was "the pride of the district, situated on a high commanding site [with] a fine view of mountains, rivers and buttes and is easily seen by strangers coming into town from the north and east." (Claude H. Kelley photo)

The inaccurate Willamette dweller probably has never been east of The Cascades in his life, or it may be, at the time of his writing, the proverbial Willamette rain or the exhaustion of navigating through constant mud has left him so depressed as to be unable to imagine ought but the blackest.[23]

The boosterism nature of *The Bulletin* was undoubtedly no different from that of other weekly newspapers throughout the western part of the United States. Cursory glances at the Bend newspaper, during the years the railway was rapidly stretching south from the Columbia River, revealed the intense expectation about the effects such an event would have on the land and the people of Central Oregon, even to the point of annoyance for those who felt that they were missing out on the excitement. A letter to the Bend newspaper in January, 1910, stated:

Will you kindly discontinue sending me *The Bulletin*. I have sold my land in Crook County and the weekly visits of *The*

Reid School, built with locally quarried stone in 1914, was named after Miss Ruth Reid, the first principal. The school was still in use in 1978.

The original Pilot Butte Inn about 1910. It was located where the Pilot Butte Inn building, constructed in 1917, stood. You can see the rock walls for which Wall Street was named. (Frances Barry photo)

Anxious spectators giving moral support to crews laying rail tracks cut into lava rock north of Bend, in 1911. (Jim Arbow photo)

Wall Street, 1911, looking south. "Bend the Beautiful" was the civic slogan of the day. Note the telephone poles. Bend was connected to Prineville by phone in 1904. In 1906 there were seven phones in Bend, and by 1917 there were 313. The first power came in 1910 from a power dam on the Deschutes River behind the old Pilot Butte Inn. (Phil F. Brogan photo)

George Palmer Putnam, publisher and owner of *The Bulletin*, 1910-1919. Putnam was the president of Pinelyn Corporation which developed the fashionable Drake Park residential area. Putnam later married Amelia Earhart, aviatrix who disappeared on a trans-world flight, 1937. The Bend Park Company, a Seattle-based company, subdivided large parcels of land in Bend and vigorously promoted sales. (Phil F. Brogan photo)

Bulletin only annoy me by reminding me of what I have lost, and that I will not see Crook County, Oregon, again.[24]

Bend grew rapidly following the completion of the railroad to the city.* The influx of people to homestead the High Desert or to work in Bend brought landscape changes which did not go unrecorded by visitors. In 1912, an insurance man visiting Bend noted:

I have formed a very high opinion of Bend's citizenship. In a town of its size, I have never met a better or more quiet, orderly and respectable people. It boasts ten saloons and five active church organizations. The town has a bright future.[25]

Thus, Bend emerged from a tent and shanty village to a more sophisticated town. As in any other growing community, there were the fashionable or more desirable parts. Park Addition became known as the Nob Hill of Bend, with new, modern residences—modern colonial style, two stories in height with basements, roofs covered with native shingles, and foundations built of pink stone.

Building materials used in the early days helped shape the city's landscape. Bend entered the stone age when it began using the pink or black stone (tuff), quarried from the banks of the Deschutes River south of town. This stone, described as making durable, handsome buildings, and absorbing little water, was used in a number of downtown buildings, including the railroad depot and Reid School, which still stand. A distinct characteristic of the stone is its peculiar property of hardening after being taken out of the quarry. When the quarry is first exposed, the stone is very soft and can be cut into with an axe. This permits easy quarrying and cheap working. Then after exposure for a short time, it becomes much harder. In 1913, a Bend city ordinance stated that all buildings within the business district were to be of fire-proof construction.

---

*The exciting story of construction of rail lines into Central Oregon is told by Phil F. Brogan in the chapter, "Battle of the Gorge," in *East of the Cascades*; and by Francis Juris and John Due, in *Rails to the Ochocos*.

Another durable building material used extensively in commercial buildings in downtown Bend was fire-made bricks. The Bend brickyard, which employed as many as twenty people, was located three miles west of Bend on what is now the Shevlin Park Road. Brick clay, 98 feet thick, had accumulated in pockets of what was possibly an old lake bed, sandwiched between underlying pumice and the surface lava rock. Fine white sand for the brick making was obtained from the Ice Caves Road south of Bend. The brick, fired with cordwood, became a status symbol in Bend in 1912 and thereafter. Buildings constructed of "Lewis" brick included the O'Donnel Building, the new Catholic Church (1919), Kenwood School, the Fire Station, and the Bend Woolen Mill. For several years Bend obtained domestic water from wells at the brickyard site, after water from the Deschutes River became contaminated by obnoxious plants at Crane Prairie Reservoir.

The growth of Bend proceeded with regard for the aesthetic attractiveness of the town, noted for its towering ponderosa pine. Attempts to preserve scenic corridors and attractive stands of pine have been successful. A letter to the Bend newspaper in 1911, signed by 25 concerned residents, spoke in favor of saving trees in Bend:

Nothing adds more to the Bend beauty than the presence of its trees. It is the thing that strikes visitors most. Bend's trees will make her famous. In other places less fortunate, fortunes are spent in an effort to save trees. Even if it costs the city a little more to preserve the trees, the extra expense is well repaid, as when it may be necessary to construct sidewalks or ditches around them. One man offered to provide a few cords of firewood rather than cut down trees. The beautiful trees at the south end of Wall Street were ruthlessly cut down. [26]

It is worth noting that in recent years, suggestions to remove the tall pines along Jones Road north of Bend to widen the highway met with organized resistance on the part of nearby residents. Even the mention of cutting down an immense, aged pine that

Passenger trains connected Bend with Fall Bridge, Washington side of the Columbia River, where main-line connections to Portland and back east could be made. In this photo (1914), the train consisted of a baggage car, rail post office, two day coaches and a sleeper. Passengers could take overnight sleeper to Bend, have the car switched at Fall Bridge and wake up at Portland. (Claude H. Kelley photo)

Bend railroad depot has been the destination for countless homesteaders and settlers. No passenger trains serve Bend at the present. Note use of local stone for the building.

Street construction on Wall in 1913. Lara's was located on the site of the J.C. Penney Store. (Phil F. Brogan photo)

Start of a "business district" near the mills on Colorado Street about 1916. (Phil F. Brogan photo)

towers over the Deschutes County Library brought forth anguished cries of protest from concerned citizens. The roots of such environmentally conscious feelings in Bend country go back nearly three quarters of a century.

Civic-minded thoughts and courtesy were extended to Bend visitors in 1912. A *Bulletin* editorial called for help in establishing a watering trough and a public hitching place to "benefit everyone, especially farmers who come in to purchase supplies and are obliged either to leave their horses standing dry, or pack water to them in a bucket."[27]

Bend's landscapes were changing quite rapidly by 1912. The original Drake Place, this "unique structure made of logs finished most artistically and surrounded by a magnificent lawn and commanding a splendid view of the river, the timber, and the mountains, was being encroached on by the growing town. A large stone building, several frame business structures, and a residence have risen on the famous old lawn that for almost a decade has been the showplace of western Crook County."[28] In 1912, several beautiful residences costing over $5,000, a dozen over $3,500, and practically all others over $1,250 had been constructed. Each new subdivision—by 1912 there were many—touted its assets to the potential purchaser. Let us examine a few claims as advertised in issues of *The Bulletin*:

Riverside and Lytle

What North Portland is to Portland, Riverside and Lytle will be to Bend. The property lies along the Deschutes River north of the business district, the Oregon Trunk and OWR&N joint track. It has its own water system and special inducements to manufacturing enterprises. Lots 50' by 140' for $100-$300. Outcropping of rocks already adapted for bungalows or smooth clear lots free from rock where gardens and lawns can be had the first year.

Center Addition

Houses mostly of the bungalow style and show up to good advantage among the juniper trees.

Kenwood

Across the river. Four blocks to the Pilot Butte Inn. Views of the town, the river and the mountains. Lots $70-$150. Water and sidewalks guaranteed. Connected to Lytle by a steel bridge.

Bend Park

Future fine residential additions to Bend. Like a beautiful park with pine trees. Winding drives and boulevards and gorgeous panoramic views of the Cascades.

Riverside Addition

Will become the factory district of Bend, the most practical and most desirable. Lots right on the banks of the Deschutes River. Near Bend's largest power plants.

Pinelyn Park*

Lots $150-$400. All lots within 3/8 mile of the business center. One half the lots have river frontage. About the only residential lots in Bend on the Deschutes. Building restrictions.

Awbrey Heights

Future high-class residential district of Bend. Commanding views of the business district and Deschutes River. New steel bridge near property. City water and electric lights in a short time.

The future of Central Oregon was seen by railroad empire builder, James J. Hill, with rosy-colored glasses in 1912. He estimated that "within five years the population of Central Oregon will be 300,000. Within ten years, it should be more than a million."[29]

S.W. Lorimer, inventor of the automatic telephone, stated,

---

* Pinelyn Park was A.M. Drake's last property, eleven acres west of the Deschutes opposite the "Boy Scouts" lodge (Bend's first schoolhouse), and the Narrows. Land was described as wooded with many handsome pines and some of the finest mountain views obtainable anywhere, as well as a beautiful view of the attractive river front side of the town. A.M. Drake had retained this property as a home site, announcing that he would build a handsome residence there and lay out elaborate grounds. Plans for the latter were perfected by Mrs. Drake and some preliminary clearing was done before the tract was sold to a corporation headed by G.P. Putnam, editor and publisher of *The Bulletin*.

Wall Street on a busy day in 1913. Almost everyone in town must have been there! People appear smartly dressed. (Phil F. Brogan photo)

Wall Street, 1978, at same location as 1913 photo. Wooden buldings seen in 1913 have long been replaced by more fire-proof construction materials. Wall Street is now one-way at this location.

The Bend Brick and Lumber Company (1916), located 2 miles west of Bend adjacent to the Shevlin Park Road, supplied countless bricks which have helped shape Bend's landscapes. On September 6, 1916, *The Bulletin* reported that the brickyard had been in operation for 4 years, and had a capacity of 60,000 bricks a day, employed a crew of 20 and had a daily payroll of $80. A well on the brickyard site later supplied water for Bend when water from the Deschutes River developed a strange taste. (Deschutes County Library photo)

Construction (using locally made bricks) of businesses on Wall Street (corner of Oregon Avenue) in 1913. (Phil F. Brogan photo)

No stream in the Northwest equals the Deschutes in its power producing possibilities. In the ten miles above Bend one could develop enough electricity to supply all Oregon. Why plants could be installed every half mile.[30]

The start of a $75,000 sewer system began in December, 1912. In the same year, a flour mill in Bend began producing "Pilot Butte Grits" from pure wheat hearts. These grits, described as being "attractive and healthful," were packaged in ten-pound sacks with colored labels bearing a print of Pilot Butte. The stimulus of the railroad helped Bend's population to boom. Whereas the population of Bend was listed as only 300 in 1904, and 536 in 1910, it had reached 1,750 by mid-1912. In addition to residences, a power dam, a flour mill, and stores, Bend began to boast several hotels. The Altamont—now a stylish apartment building on Broadway—and the Mountain View, in 1913, advertised their location on the banks of the Deschutes River:

Spend Sunday afternoon on our green lawns and cool verandah watching the clouds, the river and the mountains. Then step in to dinner.[31]

By 1915, Bend's accelerated growth was viewed with some alarm by the local newspaper. In April of that year, an editorial cautioned the city on such growth:

The town is somewhat overgrown as things now stand. We have most excellent city foundations here, but we have progressed so far already there is need for conservative development of what we already have before we launch much further into town building. In other words, Bend is like an overgrown boy just blossoming into manhood; he needs to fill out and get flesh on his bones and strengthen the strength in his muscles before he undertakes too much man's work. We need to keep the brakes or to go slow—if we can![32]

Lumber Mills Stimulate Growth

The month following this editorial, the Shevlin-Hixon Lumber Company announced its plans to build a large mill in Bend. By June, 1915, work had started on a dam at the proposed mill site just upstream from the town. Brooks-Scanlon Lumber Company almost simultaneously announced its intention to start construction of a mill in Bend. The impact of two mills was a profound one. Within two years, scores of homes were hastily erected in Bend. On January 19, 1916, *The Bulletin* ran the following advertisement and included a picture of the houses:

Build it Yourself Houses—machine sawed material numbered to correspond with plans insures a perfect fit. Knock-down homes from Portland for as low as $205—economically built homes, permanent, substantial and attractive.

So great was the influx of people into Bend that in January, 1916, despite temperatures down to -19° F, some families were forced to live in tents because of a housing shortage. During that period, the Bend Benevolent Association helped many families find better temporary quarters.

The Shevlin-Hixon and the Brooks-Scanlon lumber mills had started operations by the spring of 1916. By April of that year, Bend's population had reached 3,205. Water Tower Hill, one block east of Bend, was selected as a hospital site in November, 1916. The Bend Park Company also offered a site for a hospital, a 5-1/2-acre tract of land near the foot of Pilot Butte. It is of interest to note that although the St. Charles Hospital, razed in 1977, long occupied the Water Tower Hill site, the modern, imposing St. Charles Medical Center, which replaced the St. Charles Hospital, is now located within a short distance of Pilot Butte.

Although the Brooks-Scanlon and the Shevlin-Hixon lumber mills became prominent landscape features in Bend, one of the lesser-known pioneer industries was the Bend Juniper Products

West side of Bond Street from Oregon Avenue to Greenwood (1914). All the people in the photo appear to be men with time to gossip. (Phil F. Brogan photo)

Same location as 1914 Bond Street photo but taken in 1978. Structures in the background are Deschutes County Courthouse buildings.

A street scene on Wall Street about 1913. The street was torn up for the laying of the sewer; the pipe can be seen in the foreground. Note the fine street lights. Buildings at this time were largely built with wood. Brick building (background) is where Healey's Furniture Store is now located. (Phil F. Brogan photo)

Winter landscape, Bend Flour Mill (1920's). Wheat for the mill came from the Madras area. The mill, located on railroad spur across Wall Street was later used as a feed mill before burning down. (Claude H. Kelley photo)

Company, which produced juniper wood for pencils. This industry, established in 1919, used juniper from trees pulled by crews established in two camps between Tumalo and Deschutes Junction, to produce wooden slats for pencil makers in the United States, Germany, Austria, Japan, France, Italy and Spain. However, Central Oregon juniper, *Juniperus occidentalis*, is often stricken by an interior pocket rot. Because of financial difficulties, the pencil factory ceased operations by 1924.[33]

Another industry which flourished only a short time was the Bend Woolen Mill, which really functioned only as a knitting factory. Oregon wool yarn was received from Portland. From this yarn, starting in 1923, sweaters, socks and underwear were manufactured. Financial difficulties, however, forced the mill to close three years later. The building later functioned as a meat market, a dance hall, a grocery store, and a furniture business.[34] Today, the brick-built "Bend Woolen Mill" is a well-known tavern.

By the 1920's, many aspects of what are today's older residential areas had taken shape. Important features of house construction around 1920, which can still be seen in many parts of town, were the use of brick facing, stone-built basements or foundations, and sun porches. Many of the houses still add a distinctive character to the residential landscape.

The front porch has been described as an "American institution of high civic and moral value. It is a sign that the people who sit on it are ready and willing to share the community life of their block with their neighbors."[35] The porch became an American symbol for friendliness and propriety. It was a place to sit in the cool of the evening. It added character and size to otherwise modest homes.

Later, as the automobile came into widespread use, porches became less attractive. People became more mobile and spent less time at home. The backyard patio and garden became more fashionable, and television contributed to more inside use of the home. Yet, the landscape of Bend still reflects the fashion of half a century ago.

The accelerated growth of Bend that followed the arrival of the two large lumber mills continued during the 1920's, and the need for city planning in Bend was identified as early as 1921.[36] In 1922, 211 buildings were started in Bend, 400 in 1924, and 462 in 1925. By 1924, the city population was listed at 7759, up from the 1920 census of 5414. It reached 8821 by 1930, when Bend was widely identified as a "lumber town."

In 1937, the end of the supply of lumber for Bend mills was forecast. Dr. F.A. Silcox, United States Forest Service chief, stated that the Bend mills were overcutting their renewable supply of lumber, and he forecasted that Bend had about twenty years "to live." Strong editorials taking exception to Silcox's statement came from Salem and Eugene newspapers. The *Eugene Register-Guard*, for example, pointed out the other assets of Bend country—power from Benham Falls, more irrigation water to expand agriculture, more alfalfa and grazing land, and tourism.

Bend survived the lumber famine scare. Today, United States Forest Service and Brooks-Scanlon lands are harvested on a sustained yield basis, assuring sufficient raw material for future generations.

Although the population growth rate leveled off compared with the rapid increase experienced in the period 1916-1930, confidence in the future of the area was seen by the construction of a new Deschutes County Courthouse (1940), and an additional unit to the St. Charles Hospital (1950). The prospect of a pulp mill to provide new jobs for 700 people was announced in December, 1956. Although the Bend City Commission supported Brooks-Scanlon as the possible mill location, the pulp mill construction never materialized. In 1950, the Shevlin-Hixon mill was purchased by Brooks-Scanlon and closed. The growth of Bend stagnated for a few years, but by the late 1950's and early 1960's, Bend started to become the focal point for another type of industry—tourism.

Sewer construction on Greenwood Avenue in 1913. Pilot Butte in background. The building on the left, Hotel Oregon, the first business building to be constructed of stone in Bend, still stands. Note the railroad overpass, still a traffic hazard for vehicles with high loads. (Frances Barry photo)

Greenwood Avenue, 1977. Stone buildings constructed 60 years ago are almost lost between modern commercial buildings. Railroad underpass and Pilot Butte in background.

Oregon Avenue looking west from Bond Street in 1914, prior to the construction of the O'Kane building. (Phil F. Brogan photo)

Oregon Avenue looking west from Bond Street (1978). Most of the buildings seen in this photo have replaced structures seen in 1914 photo. On the left is the O'Kane Building.

Tourism

When the Shevlin-Hixon and Brooks-Scanlon lumber mills had reached the peak of their production in the 1930's, it was predicted that Bend's population would level off at around 8,900. Although several factors have combined to account for the population growth since the 1950's, tourism has been a factor in many land use changes in recent years.

Actually, Bend has long catered to tourists. It is difficult to say when the first tourist identified the recreational assets of the Bend country, but as early as 1900, one of the favored camping spots in the area was near the Staats store and post office, the site where the Shevlin-Hixon Company office building was later located. Here, tourists spent the night, usually sleeping in the hay in the Staats' barn.

It was not many years later that Bend earned a reputation for fine hotels, good hospitality, and accommodations. What brought early-day tourists to Bend at a time when the highways of interior Oregon alternated between dust and mud? For many years, only a trail roughly followed the present route of Highway 97. For many years, there was no Government Camp Highway, and no Santiam Pass route to Eugene. Little traffic moved over the Cascades by way of the McKenzie lava fields, even in midsummer.

Despite its isolation and travel obstacles, the town began to pride itself on its scenic attractions. By 1912, Portland residents could travel to Bend by rail for $7.45 a round trip. Noted places to visit included the ice caves "where nature manufactures ice in summer faster than a wagon can haul it away."[37] The Deschutes and the Crooked River were said to be streams where the "trout are everywhere and all hungry for the artificial fly."[38] Other tourist attractions were the lava beds, wind caves, and the Paulina Mountains. Recreational opportunities included canoeing, camping, and mountain climbing.

Bend advertised its scenic and recreational attractions at the 1915 San Francisco Exposition and included maps showing the town on the "main route" from Klamath Falls to the Columbia River and Portland. As it does today, north-south traffic to Crater Lake brought tourists through Bend. In 1916, a total of 1749 autos visited Crater Lake. It was estimated that a third of the motorists passed through Bend, many staying overnight. The city estimated that income from tourists (580 autos, 2320 people, each spending $4) brought over $8000 revenue to the city in 1916.

By the spring of 1919, the city of Bend provided camping facilities for tourists on land adjacent to the Deschutes River, donated by the Bend Company. For several years, this company had been promoting land sales in Bend. City crews transformed a heap of dirt into a grassy haven for tourists. Families brought tents, camp supplies and food, and set up housekeeping on the spot where Pioneer Park is now located. In those days, tourists could be almost certain of catching thirty, forty or more trout in the Deschutes River.

In May, 1919, *The Bulletin* noted that there was scarcely a night without a few small fires seen in the campground enclosure. Later that year, the paper called attention to the scenic assets of the Bend area:

Central Oregon is coming into its own as a country of tremendous attraction to tourists and sportsmen. As tourists are welcomed this leads to more business and more developments and a brush with the outside world.[39]

The editorial called for good roads into the mountains and the lakes. It asked residents not to catch all the fish, cautioning them to be careful with fires in the woods and to leave areas as they found them.

In the month of August, 1920, with Bend's tourist trade at its height despite a gas shortage, 180 tourists registered at the local hotels. The Pilot Butte Inn, which had opened in 1917, reported that it was mailing daily a steady number of post cards showing "scenic views of the lumber mills." Many tourists to Bend took time to tour the mill and other local industries.[40]

A 1915 view of Bond Street, looking south. A number of buggies can be seen but only one car. Structure next to land office was the Wenandy Livery Stable. (Frances Barry photo)

Bond Street, looking south from Greenwood Avenue, in 1978. Most of the buildings there in 1915 have been removed. Trailways Restaurant is where land office was located. Building now occupied by Original Joe's (second right) was standing in 1915.

Dam on the Deschutes near Newport Avenue, 1977. Pilot Butte Inn stood behind Elks Club (large building in center).

Nº 15 POWER DAM, BEND, ORE.

Wooden flume (left) led to the power plant, then a wooden building housing a single generator. Electricity from this system came to Bend in 1910. In background, buildings are along Wall Street. (Oregon Historical Society photo)

Use of the city campground increased steadily. In 1922, it was estimated that 1000 people used the facilities. Autoists were charged fifty cents a car to use the camp stoves and tables. Motor travel, though becoming more and more popular in the 1920's, was still slow compared to today's standard. One motorist reported that he made the "280 miles from McCloud, California to Bend in three days."[41] It also took motorists three days for the trip from Portland to Bend, due in part to the bad state of the Central Oregon highways.

The Dalles, Klamath Falls, and Bend commercial clubs joined to promote The Dalles-California Highway in 1925, with tourist literature showing the volcanic wonders of Deschutes County, unimpeded views of glaciers, peaks of the Cascades, the vast wheat fields of Sherman County, and the fertile lands of Wasco County. The 1920's saw the peak in the number of hotels in Bend, the start of auto cabins or tourist camps, and the first public swimming pool, which was built by A.C. Kirtsis. In 1927, Kirtsis built one of the first auto camps, north of the city campground at a site where the Bend Riverside Condominiums now overlook the Deschutes River. Auto-park accommodations usually consisted of a bed, springs and mattress, a few chipped and battered dishes, possibly a cooking utensil or so, and a wood stove that served for both heating and cooking. Charge ranged from $1 and upward for a night's stay, but the "better places" usually got up to $2 a night.

The reaction to tourism was generally positive. *The Bulletin*, in August, 1928, reported that most of the tourists visiting Bend "think enough of their experience to return next year. There are a few who aren't pleased, but generally these are the type who would suspect the government of putting bluing in Crater Lake. Most complaints are directed at the road conditions along Century Drive."[42]

By 1936, Bend boasted eleven auto camps, or auto courts as they were later called. That same year, the town was given air service to Portland twice a week. Flights took 1-1/4 hours. In May, the Santiam Pass opened for traffic. The event was celebrated by Bend and Eugene officials, with both groups

Construction of power house and storage dam (1913). Building on the right is flour mill. (Phil F. Brogan photo)

Power House (left background) is used by Pacific Power and Light Co. to generate electricity for systems serving Central Oregon. Willow trees nearly obscure the building in this 1978 photo.

lunching together in Sisters on the weekend of May 18, 1936. *The Bulletin* reported:

> . . .sightseers crossed and recrossed the Santiam Pass. Restaurant business in Bend was so heavy that a number of local restaurants were forced to call on grocerymen to open their stores to replenish depleted larders. One restaurant turned away approximately 100 people due to lack of accommodations.[43]

During and immediately after World War II, a shortage of gasoline and automobile tires curtailed travel. However, once the shortages were overcome, tourism by car grew rapidly. By the mid 1950's, some of the half dozen hotels that operated in Bend were thirty or more years old. Many of these were converted into apartments or rooming houses as motels became more fashionable for the motoring tourist. The number of motels or auto courts grew from 17 in 1946, to 25 in 1950, and 30 in 1955.

Late in 1962, the Highway 97 by-pass was opened, rerouting through traffic one mile east of downtown Bend. Landscape changes resulting from the establishment of the "by-pass" have been profound. In many respects the character of Third Street, as it is commonly known, reflects a typical commercial strip highway, found in "Anytown, U.S.A." For several miles along the elongated, busy highway, a succession of neon signs and billboards scream for tourists' and area residents' attention. Add large, sterile asphalt parking lots, utility lines, power poles, traffic lights, and an overflow of autos and trucks, and one can see that here the aesthetic image of Bend is tarnished. Admittedly there have been attempts to landscape properties in recent years. City ordinance now insists that landscaping be required of all new businesses. In places along the southern entrance to the city, tall ponderosa pines help subdue the commercial landscape. Increased tourism is to a large extent responsible for the creation of the commercial appearance of Third Street. Conspicuous along this busy highway are the motels, restaurants and gas stations. The growth of the service

View looking east from Shevlin-Hixon Mill, in 1916, to the original Brooks-Scanlon Mill. Lumber storage area is in background. Note the absence of buildings east of the mill. In August, 1916, Brooks-Scanlon had a labor force of 350 with a monthly payroll of $28,000. Shevlin-Hixon's labor force that month was 710 with a $57,400 payroll. (Phil F. Brogan photo)

Bustling mills and rows of drying lumber meant a strong economy for Bend. The mill complex, which included a sawmill, a sash and door factory, and a box factory, closed down in 1950 when the company was purchased by Brooks-Scanlon. (Phil F. Brogan photo)

industries since World War II is evident when one considers that the number of motels, restaurants, and gas stations almost doubled to approximately thirty of each.

Tourism is now much more of a year-round business than it was fifteen years ago. Until skiing became established at Bachelor Butte around 1960, the motels and restaurants had relatively little winter business. Skiing season filled the gap between the end of hunting and beginning of fishing season and brought many large motels and restaurants to Bend. The full impact of tourism on the Bend area can only be measured when one considers the growth of nearby recreational subdivisions, the planned resort communities of Sunriver and Black Butte Ranch, and the general intense interest of tourists and others in "relocating" in Bend.

Throughout the summer months in particular, the State of Oregon Employment Office and the Bend Chamber of Commerce are deluged with requests for information on employment and real estate in the Bend area. It is significant to note that many of the people writing to the Chamber of Commerce state that they had visited Bend while on vacation, that they had "fallen in love with the area" and wished to settle there. Many Californians expressed dissatisfaction with the urban environment in Southern California, citing such problems as "congestion," too many people, "smog," and "high crime rate." Bend, with its attractive landscape, its dry, sunny climate and seasonal changes, is contributing to the population redistribution in the United States. At the same time, the rapid growth of year-round tourism and the influx of new residents to the Bend country is rapidly changing the area's landscapes.

3.

DOWNTOWN BEND

The entire downtown area is neatly "contained" by the Deschutes River, Troy Field, the old hospital site, the Cascade Junior High site, and the Deschutes County Courthouse. Several landscape features distinguish this downtown area from the downtown areas of many other cities of similar size. Admittedly, in some ways, Wall Streets takes on the appearance of "Main Street, U.S.A." Parking meters, the ever-present watchdogs of precious time, stand at attention along all streets in the core area. A mixture of time-worn bricks and new facades adorn the fronts of the commercial buildings. Many kinds of stores occupy all the lower floors of buildings in the commercial district; upper floors either have false fronts, or are put to a different use from those on ground level.

Other facets of the downtown area are "uniquely Bend." Where else would one discover at the back door of an established commercial area as picturesque a landscape scene as that of tranquil Mirror Pond? From the Mirror Pond parking lot, located near the site of the A.M. Drake residence, the view to the west is impressive. In the foreground, towering ponderosa pine shade a grassy slope which, in turn, abruptly plunges down to the Deschutes River.

Unsuspecting people could be excused if they believe that the calm body of water reflecting trees and bushes is a natural lake rather than a tranquil river. Even those looking at the Deschutes

Brooks-Scanlon Mill B showing mill buildings (background), the old power-house (center) and stacks used only for emergency situations—and the new power house (left) which is able to produce considerable amounts of energy used at the plant.

Storage of logs in the Deschutes River near the Brooks-Scanlon Mill. Logs were once brought to the river by rail and stored in the Deschutes. However, because bark from the timber was silting the bottom of the Deschutes, Oregon Department of Environmental Quality now prohibits such methods of storage. (Deschutes County library photo)

River from this spot might find it difficult to believe that, upstream and downstream, this docile stream is the untamed "River of the Falls." Across Mirror Pond, many attractive lawns and spacious landscaped yards picturesquely border the west bank of the river. A rustic footbridge for pedestrians and cyclists links the "west side" of Bend with Drake Park.

The background landscape scene of downtown Bend includes the wooded slopes of the West Hills residential area, the blue, forested foothills of the Cascades, and the familiar, snow-capped peaks of the Cascades. Even the sterile streets of the core area have been beautified by the planting of young saplings that struggle to survive in the urban environment. For several years, the beautification of "Downtown Bend" and other commercial parts of the city has been accomplished by the addition of hanging flower baskets during the summer months. This project, started by the Men's Garden Club, is now continued by the Soroptomists Club with funds from public donations. Here and there on the periphery of the downtown, giant, aged ponderosa pine have managed to survive what originally must have been a pine forest.

Many aspects of the environment and the cultural atmosphere in downtown Bend contrast with that to be found along Third Street. While the latter is a typical urban strip highway, with a landscape largely geared to the motorist, the role of the pedestrian is more evident downtown. Several spacious parking lots off the edge of the core area are within 100 to 200 yards from most of the downtown area. Wide sidewalks, and friendly backdoor entrances to retail stores backing Mirror Pond parking lots, create more of a "sense of place" where men, not machines, are important.

In recent years, many small specialty stores selling hand-crafted goods have contributed to the character and friendly personality of downtown Bend. During the summer and early fall months, a Saturday Market attracts vendors and casual buyers to mingle and discuss handmade leather, jewelry, pottery, and so forth.

"Downtowns" have traditionally been the commercial and cultural heart of cities. Historically, in Bend, with the Pilot Butte Inn, downtown has been the symbolic center and gathering place for the community. However, the Third Street bypass, built in the early 1960's, drained some of the vitality from the heart of the city. The razing of the Pilot Butte Inn and the defeat of the Downtown Development Program in 1973 temporarily slowed development projects in the commercial core of Bend. This program was a detailed study of the economic and aesthetic problems and prospects of the core area, conducted by the architectural firm of Hall and Goodhue of San Francisco. Their plans, which sparked controversy over financing and property acquisition, was put to public vote and rejected.

Now there are signs of a revival for downtown Bend, with construction on the Pilot Butte Inn site, and plans for retail use of the vacant St. Charles Hospital land. When Greenwood Avenue and Wall Street, the entrance to downtown Bend, were realigned in 1976, a small triangle of land, reflecting cooperation of several public agencies, created a mini-park, Brandis Square. This was named and dedicated in November, 1976, in memory of Richard W. Brandis, community leader and former mayor of Bend. It is important that any future plans for the heart of Bend consider the role of the pedestrian, acknowledge the scenic site along the Deschutes River and, overall, retain a "sense of place," an area where the quality of human awareness is important.

Pilot Butte Inn

Although The Pilot Butte Inn is no longer part of the Bend landscape, its historical importance, its reputation, and the memories it evokes are justification enough for its inclusion in any book that focuses on the history and geography of Bend. It was January 1, 1916, that Phillip R. Brooks—a distant relative of the Brooks family connected with the Brooks-Scanlon mill—announced that he was ready to go ahead with the construction of a hotel that would accommodate business visitors to Bend. The building was to reflect the Swiss Chalet style. A Portland architect, John E. Tourtelhothe, drew plans for the three-story building. Construction began in September, 1916, on the site of the original Pilot Butte Inn, built at the turn of the century.

The new Pilot Butte Inn was dedicated on St. Patrick's Day, 1917. A special train from Portland brought notables and newspapermen to Bend. A reception from 4 to 6 p.m. was followed by an evening dinner held in shifts from 6 to 9 p.m., to accommodate the huge throng. Dancing until midnight followed the dinner. There was another reception until 4 a.m., but as 1917 was the era of prohibition, no "drinking" was allowed.

Native stone was used for the ground-level story of the Inn, with pine timbers, cut at the local sawmills, on the upper two stories. Initially, the extensions to the building in the 1920's and 1930's added about an additional 200 rooms. One of the famous features of the Inn was a 16 x 6-foot picture window overlooking the Deschutes River and framing a panorama of mountain peaks. The glass for the window was shipped in from France. Valuable oil paintings and antique pieces were part of the interior decor. Outside, landscaped grounds included rock gardens and 500 imported alpine plants. Vines eventually spread over part of the Inn's exterior and, in season, bright flowers bloomed in window boxes made of scooped-out logs.

The Pilot Butte Inn quickly got a fine reputation. A report by a Portland visitor, in 1919, stated:

The Inn gives the tourist a hearty welcome and comfortable service. The visitor is greeted in the morning at breakfast with a wide expanse of snow-capped peaks and from the great plate-glass windows in the dining room, can look upon the cool loftiness of the Three Sisters, the Bachelor and Old Broken Top.[44]

For many years, the Pilot Butte Inn stood as the main cultural landmark in Bend. It long served as a focal point for visitors to the city. It catered to the social needs of Bend residents, with

Giant log stacker carries a load toward the Brooks-Scanlon small log mill. Steam in background is from the power house. (Brooks Scanlon Corp. photo, Bend)

Left: Disused railroad grade between Bend and the Shevlin Park area. Decaying wooden ties once supported steel rails which formerly carried lumber-laden trains to the Brooks-Scanlon Mill, extended across Tumalo Creek on a trestle, and as far west as the Sisters country. The grade was used until logs were brought into Bend by truck. Right: Arnold Ice Cave, located 10 miles southeast of Bend, supplied residents of Bend with ready-made ice during hot summer months. Here, cut ice is transported down chute from cave entrance.

Mirror Pond, 1978. View from parking lot adjacent to downtown Bend, looking west across to Drake Park (left) and forested foothills of Cascades (background).

Deschutes River from A.M. Drake residence in 1905. At that time the river was in its natural channel. This same channel today is hidden by the deceptive tranquility of Mirror Pond. Note the rather untamed state of the vegetation along the stream banks in 1905 compared to 1978. (Oregon Historical Society photo)

balls, banquets, conventions, art shows, weddings, and concerts. Indeed Bend was the Pilot Butte Inn and, seemingly, the two could not exist without each other. The Inn hosted such distinguished visitors as Eleanor Roosevelt, former President Herbert Hoover, and humorist Irvin S. Cobb, who stated that the Inn was the finest for any small town in the United States.

The Brooks' estate was sold in 1946, at a time when hotels everywhere in the country were competing with the rapidly growing motel business. The Pilot Butte Inn fell into hard times. Taxes became overdue, and the structure lacked maintenance, which led to a deterioration of the building. The Inn was sold and resold several times over the years, and the last paying guest was in 1965. However, despite the deteriorating structural condition, the historical importance of the building, as well as nostalgia and attachment, was strong enough to prompt CORDCO (Central Oregon Resource Development Corporation) to attempt to save the Inn, and to include its restoration as part of a 19-acre riverfront development. Although CORDCO collected $30,000, and the Pilot Butte Inn was included in the National Register of Historic Places, the building was doomed.

Demolition began, June 18, 1973, but not before many local citizens were given a last chance to purchase souvenirs. Everything of practical and sentimental value was bought. Removed from the hotel before the steel demolition ball went to work was the huge stone fireplace—carefully marked to be rebuilt at a later date—the maple floor, a wrought-iron gate to the garden, room keys, chain locks, and so forth. As soon as all the collectable items had been removed from the building, the wrecking ball started its task. Even the beautiful June weather could not remove the gloom, as many bystanders watched this major cultural landmark crumple to a pile of rubble in but a few days.

The story of the Pilot Butte Inn is not quite finished. In 1976, an historical metal marker was attached to the wall surrounding the vacant site. The Pacific Northwest Bell Company, owner of the site, has completed offices and other phone facilities. In recognition of the Pilot Butte Inn, the metal marker was prominently placed on the wall near the entrance and the whole new modern structure is known as the Pilot Butte Administration Building. No matter how attractive the new building is, however, it will likely not match the elegance, charm and impact of the hotel which long occupied that historical site.

The Pine Tavern Restaurant

Now that the Pilot Butte Inn has been demolished, there is no other building in downtown Bend that is as well known as the Pine Tavern. This noted restaurant, sought by tour groups and families visiting Bend, and patronized daily by local businessmen and shoppers, is nestled between two small, attractive gift shops on Brooks Street, just one short block west of Wall Street.

Geographical, cultural and culinary factors combine to make the Pine Tavern what it now is. Usually, the backyards of restaurants border depressing litter-strewn alleys. The Pine Tavern's "backyard" is an attractive pine-shaded garden and lawn area overlooking peaceful Mirror Pond, and across to the established spacious residences bordering the Deschutes River.

The Pine Tavern's much sought-after dining place is the garden room at the rear of the restaurant. Here, diners can look across the tranquil setting described above, framed by the snow-capped peaks of the Cascades. Stately pine trees tower over the restaurant. Indeed, two huge Ponderosa pines are part of the inside decor of the dining room, which was built around their great trunks. Their towering presence adds an impressive touch of nature to the room.

The restaurant is in easy walking distance from free parking near Mirror Pond, and within two blocks of banks, offices, and numerous stores. With limited parking adjacent to the Pine Tavern, the role of the automobile along Brooks Street is less apparent than is typical of most downtown areas, and pedestrian traffic in the vicinity is quite heavy.

Pilot Butte Inn (1930). The putting green in the foreground was later the site of a Standard gas station and is now the location of a parking lot for Brandis Drug Store. (Oregon Historical Society photo)

Interior of the Pilot Butte Inn, about 1920. The photo reveals many of the elegant furnishings which decorated the Inn. (Oregon Historical Society photo)

The Pine Tavern opened in November, 1935, with around 800 people attending an "open house." Today, the restaurant employs about 45 workers, most of them full time. For 32 years, it was operated by Maren Gribskov, and it was during those years that the restaurant developed a reputation for fine food. The forerunner of the Pine Tavern was the OIC Cafeteria, operated in Bend from 1919 by Maren Gribskov and her partner, Martha Conklin. The present owner, Winn Roley, still uses many of Maren Gribskov's recipes, plus some of her own for variety, and insists on keeping the Pine Tavern's image as a friendly restaurant. This apparently is the secret of its success.

4.

LANDMARKS

Pilot Butte

Rising 500 feet over the midstate plateau, Pilot Butte is one of the major landmarks dominating the skyline east of town. This old grass-and-juniper.covered cinder cone, perhaps 50,000 or more years old, has been a beacon for travelers seeking either a crossing on the Deschutes River, or the town located at this crossing. "Ascending from this spot, following a draw west and south of Taylor Butte, the emigrants struck easy travel, but another day stretch. Their guides were the Three Sisters, and later Pilot Butte, near what is now the city of Bend. Original surveys of the Alfalfa area show old tracks going almost due west toward Pilot Butte; the thin-dim trace is labeled "Old Emigrant Road." Later, it became the "Old Bear Creek Road."[45]

Few major emigrant trains actually crossed the High Desert and approached Pilot Butte from the east; most early migrants into the Bend area traveled from the south. If anything, Pilot Butte is a clearer landmark when seen from south of Bend than from the east. Accoring to one version of the story, Pilot Butte was also a landmark used in attempts to pinpoint the location of the lost "Blue Bucket Mine" (1845):

Saturday Market held on grassy banks of the Deschutes attracts a leisurely crowd of shoppers to look over a variety of local handmade goods.

Bend's Pine Tavern on Brooks Street, noted for its fine food and garden restaurant room at the rear overlooking peaceful Mirror Pond. Note that the architectural style is more akin to an old English inn than to a restaurant in Western America.

The second day after finding the gold, they were shown Pilot Butte by an Indian, and as they only traveled about 12 miles per day it could not be more than 20 or 25 miles from that point. They reached the Deschutes River, where the town of Bend is now located. If I were going to try to find the place again, I would go to the summit of Pilot Butte and look to the Southeast and see what point in the mountains in that direction it would be possible for them to have sighted Pilot Butte.[46]*

Today, Pilot Butte is not only designated as a State of Oregon Park, but is and has long been, a feature of Bend's landscape that deserves special description. The name "Red Butte" appeared on maps of Oregon printed in 1887. By then the cinder cone was also named Pilot Butte. Before the turn of the century, this name was one of several geographical names given to the small village, which later grew up to be what is now the city of Bend. While the name *Pilot Butte* did not become permanently attached to the community developing near its western base, the Pilot Butte Inn long served travelers and citizens of Bend as a nationally famous place of hospitality. Two schools—a grade school and a junior high—located on the northern flanks of the volcanic butte, were named "Pilot Butte." The grade school has now been renamed the Juniper Elementary School. Nearby, a large residential area and a cemetery bear the name Pilot Butte.

Israel Russell, in describing the geology of Central Oregon in 1905, singled out Pilot Butte as a conspicuous landmark noted for its conical shape and steep sides.[47] Russell observed the reddish scoriaceous lava near the summit, a distinctive feature of Pilot Butte when seen from the Greenwood Avenue approach. Any crater that may have existed on the summit of Pilot Butte, Russell added, had long since disappeared.

The panorama from the top of Pilot Butte is still impressive today, as it must have been for tourists and early-day Bend residents. In viewing Bend and the surrounding countryside from Pilot Butte, W.D. Cheney described the landscapes in 1918:

It is the most beautiful setting for an inland city that could be imagined. Best seen from Pilot Butte, 600 feet above the town, the site of the city is a level valley in a cleft of pine-clad hills. Beyond the green hills are other hills that are blue. Those are also covered with forest, and they roll higher and higher, hill beyond hill, and bluer and bluer, until they end in the snow-capped peaks of the Cascade Mountains. The little valley below is openly planted, like a park, with small pines and grey junipers, half hiding the buildings of the town. Here and there the river flashes in the sunshine, and off at the left, the blue smoke of the mills rises lazily in the still, cool air.

The air is so keen and still that every distant sound in the valley below comes up clear and musical, like the stroke of a bell, and yet the low hum of the mills, the sound of busy hammers, the barking of a dog, and the whir of automobiles, only seem to make the stillness more profound. . . . We look off to the east and stretching away as far as the eye can reach we see level land, all irrigated, with here and there white specks that are houses and green squares that are farms.

We have just come from the north through twenty miles of irrigation. We now see irrigation clear to the horizon—northern, east and southern. We know that beyond those irrigated lands to the east and south are millions of acres of future grain lands.

We know that back of us are countless miles of virgin forest—forests of pine, the wood fast becoming so rare—and we realize that we are standing at the distribution center of a county so rich in resources that a city, not a town, but a city must some day be built here.[48]

A city, indeed, was built, and Pilot Butte is one of the best vantage points to witness the continued growth of that city. Many of the new subdivisions scattered through the pine and juniper are, in places, barely visible during daylight hours, but after dark, countless twinkling lights are a better indicator of the area's rapid population growth. Pilot Butte has stood its ground in the wake of land developments around its red-and-black cindery flanks. Hastened by a decision to locate a new ultra-modern hospital east of "The Butte," the pattern has been set for construction of medical offices, residential subdivisions,

Pilot Butte seemingly dead-ends Greenwood Avenue. Pilot Butte is a state park, its summit accessible by a spiral, paved road.

Bend from Pilot Butte in the mid 1970's. Cascade peaks in background (right to left) are the North, Middle, South Sister, Broken Top and Ball Butte. (Oregon State Highway photo)

and—along parts of the Burns Highway—new commercial activity, all on the "desert" side of Bend.

As recently as the 1950's, old-timers recall that there were few buildings between Third Street and Pilot Butte. In another quarter of a century, it will not be difficult to visualize Pilot Butte as being a frequently visited but uninhabited "island" rising out of a sea of urbanization which laps away at its base.

Pilot Butte has not always been treated with respect by man. Ugly scars are cut deeply into all but the western slopes. While present-day, environmentally conscious people may condemn the misuse of Pilot Butte, practical-minded citizens in 1914—confronted by streets alternately dusty or muddy—saw solutions within their nearby volcanic cinder cone. They should be laid with cinders. "Before eight o'clock the cinder pit at the bottom of Pilot Butte was operating full time with twenty volunteer shovels filling the ten wagons as fast as they appeared.[49]

For several years, cinders from the south, east, and north sides were excavated from the butte. Portions of the Bend-Burns Highway were laid with cinders from the northern slopes. The Bend Senior High School running track, which is the present site of the Bi-Mart Store, also received a mixture of Pilot Butte cinders.

The highway that spirals up Pilot Butte was started in June, 1922. By July 3, a Ford equipped with a six-speed transmission ascended the narrow, unsafe road. Later that month, the new road was used by cars every evening, all proceeding cautiously to avoid vehicles coming down. Coasting down the Pilot Butte road on a bicycle became a new sport enjoyed by Bend boys, even though the climb back up was a stiff one. Two years later, in 1924, the road to the top of Pilot Butte was widened so that two cars could safely pass anywhere. In 1928, a new highway was completed, along with the use of local lava rock for a wall around the summit road.

As expected, auto access to the summit of Pilot Butte opened up the panorama to tourists. So impressed was a visitor from Chicago that he immediately stated his intent to live in Bend. A

Pilot Butte makes an excellent viewpoint for observing the growth of Bend and resulting landscape changes. View (top) looking northeast toward Powell Buttes (background) was taken in the early 1960's. (US Forest Service photo) View below was taken in 1978. Large structure (center) is St. Charles Medical Center. New residential developments at base of Pilot Butte will house several thousand people within the next few years.

Bend from Pilot Butte about 1912. Greenwood Avenue is now located where "trail" is visible in center of photo. Railroad depot and "Greenwood" underpass are also seen. (Phil F. Brogan photo)

St. Charles Medical Center, Bend. This $12 million six-story building rising over sagebrush and juniper trees has 164 beds but is designed for expansion to total 500 beds. Each room has a picture window that must raise patient's spirits, with panoramic views across forests to the Cascade Mountains or over a juniper landscape to the Ochocos.

post card displaying a view of Bend was addressed to his wife in Chicago with the note, "This is it!" How many tourists have said those same words!

On September 30, 1928, several hundred citizens met at the top of Pilot Butte and listened to the dedication of the volcanic landmark as a state park, given to Oregon in memory of Terrence H. Foley, early-day civic leader of Bend, and past owner of Bend Water, Light and Power Company. Friends of Mr. Foley purchased the park and presented it to the state in his memory.[50]

On November 14, 1944, the name "Pilot Butte" was given to a ship launched from the Kaiser Company, Swan Island Shipyard, Portland. During World War II, the butte served as a location for a radio set-up in connection with plane operation from Redmond. And, over the years, Pilot Butte has had its share of unusual attempts to use its summit or steep cindery slopes. In September, 1923, a Ku Klux Klan ceremony was performed on the summit, with the lighting of a flaming cross. In April, 1927, an unusual golf "challenge game," from Greenwood Avenue to the summit of Pilot Butte and back, was decided when Frank Prince defeated Carl Johnson, 33-41.

Late fall, in 1963, saw the beginning of clearing brush and developing the northwest slope of Pilot Butte, in preparation for a ski run and ski jump facility to be used for the Pacific National Ski Association Junior National Championship. At that time, the Skyliners, recognizing the unreliability of winter snow in Bend, planned on using artificial snow and installing lights for night skiing. The Skyliners had been founded in the early 1920's to assist search and rescue operations in the Cascades, but later concentrated on ski activities in the Bend area.

Work on the 150' x 750'-long ski run, and a 50-meter ski jump, got underway in September, 1964. The following March, snow was hauled in from the Tumalo Falls area, and spread over the northern slope by volunteers. Limited use was made of the ski facilities and Bend's attempt to be the only city in the

Pacific Northwest with its own ski run and jump met with failure. During July, 1967, the ski jump was removed from the butte.

Meanwhile, during the spring of 1965, a rumor that Pilot Butte was "for sale" led to interest in the purchase of Bend's celebrated hilltop. A Portland man mailed a check for $398 in care of *The Bulletin*, for the volcano, stating that he simply wished to have a mountain for himself. Another person, from Lake Oswego, Oregon, indicated that he wished to lease the butte, charging admission to the public to pay for upkeep of the historic and scenic site.[51]

Today, Pilot Butte State Park is open (without charge) to Central Oregonians and visitors to the area. A trip to Bend is hardly complete without a journey to the top. Morning views of the Cascades, their snowfields and glaciers glistening in the sunlight, are perhaps the most breathtaking. As the day wears on and the sun crosses the heavens and lowers toward the western horizon, the sharpness of the lands to the east comes into focus as shadows from rimrocks and volcanic buttes stretch across the desert landscapes. Finally, as dusk descends on Central Oregon, the Cascade skyline silhouettes against the fading light to the west. During thunderstorms, "The Butte" often becomes a popular, if unsafe, vantage point for storm watchers.

Awbrey Heights

Awbrey Heights is locally more commonly called Awbrey Butte. U.S. Geological Survey maps show "Awbrey Heights" and "Awbrey Butte." Either way, it is a deceptively large, extinct volcano dominating the skyline immediately northwest of Bend. This tree-covered butte, elevation 4234 feet and rising 600 feet above the city of Bend, was named after a pioneer Central Oregon stockman, Marshall C. Awbrey.

Although Awbrey Heights affords several vantage points giving excellent views over Bend, the Paulinas, Ochocos, and the Cascades, there is not the instant 360-degree panorama that

Looking north from Pilot Butte in 1978. Beyond the subdivisions are juniper lands and irrigated acreages extending to Redmond.

Bend is growing around the base of Pilot Butte on all sides. View looking northwest was taken in 1978. In background is Black Butte.

It now may be difficult to visualize Pilot Butte as a ski jump site, but with the right slope and snow delivered by truck, the combination works even if only on a temporary basis. (Bill Van Allen photo)

Pilot Butte from Greenwood Cemetery, showing gash in south side where cinders were excavated for use on Bend streets half a century ago.

is available at the more easily accessible Pilot Butte. The top of Awbrey Heights is a series of false peaks spanned by saddles. Geologists recognize several extinct vents along the summit ridge. It is on these rocky promontories that hikers are rewarded with the far-reaching vistas mentioned above.

In the author's research through seventy years of issues of *The Bulletin*, he found few references to Awbrey Heights. The morning view from the "Westside Hilltop," as it was called, was described in May, 1919. In that newspaper article, some of the key landscape features noted were the scattered farmhouses to the northeast, the snow-capped Cascade peaks to the west and, below, the town of Bend, almost obscured by trees.

Also in 1919, plans were made for a scenic road to wind back and forth along the slopes of the heights, and for a 50-foot fire lookout tower to be built on the summit. For many years, huge flocks of sheep used to pass through Bend on their way to summer pastures in the Cascade country. In 1928, *The Bulletin* reported that 16,000 sheep crossed Portland Avenue bridge, headed west on Saginaw, then up Awbrey Heights, damaging lawns and gardens and leaving dust clinging to houses and trees.[52] It should be noted that, in 1929, a new bridge across the Deschutes River north of Bend was used to handle the movement of sheep "to avoid the woolies destroying lawns and gardens in the Awbrey Heights section of town."

Over the years, Awbrey Heights has been selectively logged, but nature has usually managed to restore the appearance of a natural landscape, except for a legacy of dirt roads. Most of the cultural impacts on Awbrey Heights have occurred on the southwestern flanks. Residential construction crept up the lower slopes as long ago as 1916. However, it was only in relatively recent years that the urban landscape of the West Hills—as the southern slopes of Awbrey Heights are known—has developed.

Much of the real estate on Awbrey Heights exchanged hands in 1957, when 310 acres of undeveloped property were disposed of in a public auction for $7,470.[53] It is interesting to note that that amount now would not pay for any one of the developed lots located high in the West Hills. Today, a network of roads and an increasing number of homes have changed the landscape in this part of Bend. In addition, apartment houses, a United States Forest Service Silviculture Laboratory, two city of Bend water reservoirs, and farther west, Central Oregon Community College add diversity to the residential setting. Many of the West Hills homesites provide spectacular views of Bend, the Paulina Mountains to the south, Pine Mountain to the southeast, and in many instances, parts of the Cascade skyline to the west.

Plans for the "subdivision" of most of the 2,200 acres of land on Awbrey Heights are in process. Brooks Resources of Bend, which owns 1,800 acres, completed a "site inventory" during the period, 1971 to 1977. The current plan for Awbrey Heights includes common areas and parks, encompass some 600 acres. The remaining 1,400 acres, according to the plan, will accommodate some 3,000 to 4,000 dwelling units by the turn of the century.[54]

Central Oregon Community College

Over a quarter of a century ago, on April 28, 1949, to be exact, the idea of college-level training to be offered in Bend was formulated. Today, Central Oregon Community College, situated on the rocky western flanks of Awbrey Heights, just two miles from downtown Bend, has one of the most scenic and picturesque college campuses in the West.

The many steps from a post-World War II dream to the physical reality of a campus did not come easily. At first, college classes were held at the old Bend High School—later Cascade Junior High—and, for the first year of operations, 1949, the four instructors shared their teaching duties between two communities, Bend and Klamath Falls. Enrollments dropped from 107 students, in the fall term of 1949, to 58 in spring quarter, but the college survived and, through the dedication of Dr. Don P. Pence, plans for a building program were established.

Location of the campus had originally been planned for five acres adjacent to the new Bend Senior High School. In 1960, alternate sites, one near the Redmond Airport and another on 160 acres south of the Powell Butte Grange Hall, were offered. Yet another site, a compromise in a Bend-Redmond fight over a location, was considered when Dr. Pence suggested that the college be located at Deschutes Junction, midway between Bend and Redmond. By late 1961, Bend was selected as the location for the college, with four potential sites to be considered: north of Pilot Butte, Awbrey Heights, south of Bend on the east bank of the Deschutes River, and near the Lelco Plant adjacent to the Bend High School.

A 140-acre tract on Awbrey Heights was finally established as the campus site, on land donated by Mr. and Mrs. Robert Coats, Elaine Mooers and Dr. J.C. Vandevert, of Bend. In June, 1963, students proposed the campus be named "College of the Cascades" and unsuccessfully petitioned the board for the renaming of the College.[55]

A master plan for the campus site was designed by the college architects, Wilmsen, Endicott, and Unthank of Portland, and construction of four buildings got underway in 1963.

The Bulletin, in reporting on the site as construction started, noted:

In an area covered by scattered pines, bitterbrush and sage only a few months ago, the framework of structures that will form the nucleus of the new junior college is rearing above trees which will be a permanent part of the campus scenery. To the west loom the Three Sisters, with snow-capped Bachelor Butte impressive as a southern anchor for the great chain of volcanic mountains.[56]

The initial nucleus of four one-story buildings, each housing classrooms and faculty offices, was completed by the fall of 1964. The campus added a student union (1965) and a library (1966). The College was formally dedicated, November 11, 1965, with Governor of Oregon, Mark Hatfield, the principal speaker. In 1967, Dr. Frederick H. Boyle succeeded Dr. Pence as president of Central Oregon Community College and, beginning in 1969, a new building program was initiated. Today, the park-like campus has twelve major buildings which serve about 1500 students in the vocational-technical and the transfer programs.

Many natural and cultural features combine to create an attractive campus. While the steep slopes of walkways between buildings may be tiring to the students as they move from class to class, each level offers a series of panoramic views of the Cascade Mountains. Outcropping of volcanic rock mixed in with juniper and ponderosa pine, bitterbrush and sagebrush, all typical of this part of Central Oregon, were the basic geological and botanical endowments the architects had to work with.

The campus itself and the views from it change with different weather conditions. On clear days that follow a mountain snowfall, the Cascade skyline appears closer and even more distinct than usual. A snowfall on campus brings an added charm to the campus scene, especially when a deep blue sky serves as a backdrop to the bright green pine needles and the dull green juniper boughs bedecked with snow. By way of contrast, warm, sunny days in late spring or early fall bring a rejuvenation in the outdoor scene at the college. The spacious sloping lawns become informal lecture and discussion "rooms." Well-fed ground squirrels and striped chipmunks add character to the campus as they playfully scurry over and under rocks, seeking handouts from "brown baggers" and chattering excitedly to anyone who wants to listen. Raucous jays, their blue plumage flashing in the pine, frequently compete for attention with their unmelodious squawk.

Perhaps one of the most inspiring views from the campus, and there are many contenders for this distinction, is the vista from the top of the campus as the sun is setting behind the sharp form of the Cascade peaks. If atmospheric conditions are right, the kaleidoscope of cloud and sky colors helps make the panorama a breath-taking sight from this college on the hill.

Cascade skyline and forest foreground provide a scenic backdrop to COCC campus. Larger building in center is the college library. COCC has about 1400 full-time students. In addition, about 2300 part-time students take non-credit classes throughout the college district, which extends from Warm Springs to Christmas Valley. (COCC photo)

Mirror Pond water pageant (1959), once held annually in July, attracted crowds of over 10,000 to Bend to witness the water-borne floats. Floats were illuminated and after passing through a large arch, drifted down the Deschutes. (Bill Van Allen photo)

5.

PARKS

Bend will grow up in the virgin forest, and it would be a fine thing to pick upon a suitable location right now for a permanent public park so that we, when we grow up and become a large-sized spot on the map, we can invite distinguished visitors to our beautiful little city and point with pride to our park systems and streets. We don't need it now because the country is all park; but in a few years from now we, in our old age,—we can be very thankful that we had foresight enough to plan a pleasant place in which to spend a Sunday afternoon with our grandchildren. . . .[57]

Those words were written over three-quarters of a century ago, when Bend was but a mere village. Today, Bend can boast some twenty parks ranging from vest-pocket size to giant 388-acre Shevlin Park. How fortunate for Bend residents and visitors to the city that many years ago Bend's citizens had the foresight and determination to set aside or procure parts of the city for its parks! The many fine parks greatly enhance the urban landscape, as well as providing common open spaces for play areas, picnics, strolling, and other uses.

One of the first parks to be created in Bend took shape on "water tower hill," where St. Charles Hospital was later built. April 20, 1916, was declared to be "Park Day" by the Bend mayor, J.A. Eastes. School closed for half a day, and high school boys worked on the hill all afternoon. Stores and businesses closed early, and all able-bodied men were expected to report and "raise a few blisters." Loose rocks were removed and grass seed sown. Swings for children, benches for all, and a stand for a summer concert were constructed. Throughout the evening, the Bend band played, and a picnic supper was served by the ladies.[58] The community spirit displayed that day led to a series of annual spring clean-up days, with contests in lawn growing and gardening.

Drake Park and Mirror Pond

Drake Park, which borders the east side of the Deschutes River along Riverside Boulevard, is undoubtedly one of Bend's most scenic assets. Mirror Pond, a placid section of the Deschutes only two blocks from downtown Bend, was created in 1909, when a power dam backed up the swift-flowing river, which previously had been contained in a narrow channel. Close scrutiny of the Deschutes from the Drake Park footbridge will reveal the location of the old river channel, a channel which looks deceptively tame but in fact has claimed several lives.

Drake Park has had a long and interesting history. In pioneer days, part of two homesteads, dating back to the end of the nineteenth century, occupied the present Drake Park site. On one of the homesteads, a one-room 24' x 40' log cabin was built in 1902, at a cost of $1000. This cabin was the first school within Bend's city limits, although a school on the John Sisemore ranch south of the city operated in the 1880's. The old log cabin in Bend also held the first formal church services in Bend, and housed *The Bulletin* in 1903. Before it eventually fell into disrepair, the log cabin was a meeting place for Boy Scouts. Now marking the approximate site of the log cabin is a stone erected by the Daughters of the American Revolution.

While most of the land along the east bank of the Deschutes River in Bend was platted—and later used for a lumber mill, residences, and businesses—the Drake Park area was held by the

Bend Company in reserve, possibly for homesites or for anticipation of future industrial development. Fortunately for Bend, nothing came of either plan. In December, 1919, a *Bulletin* editorial called for the city to purchase the property. Early in 1921, the Bend Company offered to sell the vacant 10.4 acres of riverside land to the City of Bend, and the city accepted the offer on March 1, 1921. A clean-up of unsightly weeds, dead logs in the river, and rocks along the banks then started the task of creating a park which later (1927) was named in honor of Alexander M. Drake, the founder of Bend. Over the following years, beautification of the park continued with the seeding of grass (1929), the installation of tennis courts (1923), a grandstand, the planting of maple trees that now line the park (1929), and in 1953, a rustic footbridge over the Deschutes River.

In 1933, the idea of a water carnival on Mirror Pond brought forth the following *Bulletin* editorial, which not only supported the idea of a water pageant but, at the same time, commented on the beauty and setting of Bend's two riverside parks.

Congratulations to members of Bend's Fourth of July committee who have decided to use the Mirror Pond as a setting for a unique feature of this city's projected two-day celebration, a water carnival. The quiet stretch of water between the Drake Park footbridge and the power dam forebay, flanked on one side by aged pines and on the other by homes with lawns extending to the river edge, has possibilities which we believe, have never been fully realized.

On the University of Oregon campus at Eugene, one of the highlights of the annual junior week-end program is a canoe fete, on a narrow, winding millrace. Thousands of people crowd to the brink of the little stream, diverted from the Willamette near Springfield, and watch the decorated floats as they drift lazily under overhanging branches. It is a scene long to be remembered—a scene frequently recalled by students years after they have forgotten shortcuts in calculus and methods of finding algebraic expansions.

But, we believe, conditions in Bend are ideal for an impressive water fete. And the entire population of Central

Oregon can have grandstand seats in Drake Park. In the July twilight, with the Sisters, Broken Top and Bachelor outlined against the glow of fading day, the view of decorated, illuminated floats drifting north toward the Drake Park bend, and around the Hosch point, should be impressive. Certain members of the water carnival committee have grasped the possibilities of the broad Mirror Pond and are working out features which should make the fete a memorable one.

Consider the "fadeout," as planned by W.E. Searcy of the Fourth of July Committee. Down from the Drake Park footbridge, in single line, will come the decorated floats, many of them with groups of musicians aboard. As the floats drift into the power dam forebay, they will disappear under a huge, artificial rainbow, created by varicolored lights playing on an arch of water thrown over the river by a fire department pumper. That "fadeout," the climax of Bend's Fourth of July celebration, should long remain in the memory of thousands who will watch the water show from the Drake Park bank.

In its Mirror Pond, that silent, seemingly motionless "lake" in the heart of the city, Bend has an attraction which should be used at every opportunity, as a show place. In most cities of the state, with rivers within their boundaries, the banks of the streams are almost universally unsightly. Dirty docks, unkept storage plants, rotting wharfs—such are the common views. But in Bend, the river, held captive momentarily to serve mills and power plants, is treated as a thing sacred. Two parks, Drake and Pioneer, flank its eastern bank. Shadows of virgin pines stretch over the surface of the mirror pond and at night the lights of homes are reflected from the temporarily imprisoned water.

Bend invites the entire state to join in its Fourth of July celebration and to remain for what we predict will prove the finest and most impressive feature of the celebrations.[59]

Ten thousand people, it was estimated, watched the 1933 water pageant. The mass of humanity deeply fringed both sides of the Deschutes from the Drake Park footbridge north to the lawn in front of the Masonic Hall (previously A.M. Drake's house—now the site of Mirror Pond parking lot).

Bend had long been noted for its Fourth of July celebrations. One of the first Independence Day festivities, in 1903, in which around 300 people participated, featured a baseball game between Bend and Prineville, foot and bicycle races, at least $50 worth of fireworks arranged by the Bend Mercantile, and grand balls held in the evenings of July 3 and 4. The bills for all of the events totaled $100.

In 1907, an Independence Day trout feed was staged on the banks of the cool Deschutes. Three thousand trout were barbecued and served. Joining in the 1907 trout feed and program were scores of people from Prineville, who came in their buggies and wagons and camped under the pines. They came partly to support their ball team, which won from Bend, 15 to 0, and partly to partake of the big trout caught from the Deschutes.

The Mirror Pond water pageant established itself as a traditional way to celebrate the Fourth of July in Bend, for many years. The evening beauty of the 1939 pageant was reported in *The Bulletin*:

As the queen's float reached its royal reviewing stand near a river fountain that shot a geyser. . .a moon just past its full phase eased into the eastern skies, rising over the top of Pilot Butte. During the final phase of the pageant, the July moon, tinting the edges of a few lingering clouds, played an important part in the colorful setting.[60]

After World War II, the water pageant on Bend's Mirror Pond continued for several years. Each year, thousands of people flocked to Drake Park and lined the banks of the Deschutes to witness the Parade of Floats. The pageant, however, did not continue without problems. Financial losses and insufficient help, not only to construct the floats but also to remove the debris from Mirror Pond after the pageant, contributed to the feeling that many Bend residents were "tired of arches and floats.[61] The last water pageant was staged in late July, 1965. In recent years, various other forms of Independence Day celebrations—displays, chicken barbecues, bands, concerts, and other events, climaxed by spectacular fireworks displays, continued to bring large crowds to Drake Park.

Drake Park has maintained its beauty over the years. Indeed, as large urban areas have grown unwieldly and unattractive, often destroying the best natural spots, including river banks within their boundaries—Drake Park, bordering the quietly flowing Deschutes and within walking distance to the central business district, has become more and more a place of charm.

The park, however, has had to withstand shouts of "progress." In order to construct more stands to accommodate extra seating for the Mirror Pond water pageant, a suggestion was made that fill be used on the natural lava outcrop at the point where the river bends to the north. In 1952, a proposal to replace the rustic wooden footbridge across the Deschutes River by a bridge, to carry vehicular traffic from Nashville Avenue through Drake Park, was defeated.

Today, Mirror Pond's problems are largely geological and botanical. Depositions of silt and sediment in the pond are building up wherever the velocity of the Deschutes is slowed. In several places, it is not unusual to see ducks and swans literally standing on the silt in the river. Aquatic growth has become a concern where siltation has almost reached the surface of the stream. Various attempts to clear the weeds, including almost draining the Deschutes, have not been very successful.

Despite the ecological concern for the future of Mirror Pond, Drake Park continues to be a year-round mecca for Bend residents and tourists. Visitors to the park look across the Deschutes to attractive homes on the west bank. Their well-established lawns and gardens add an elegant character and color to the Bend city landscapes. These homes are among the most prestigious in Bend.

During warm summer days, the tall cinnamon-bark ponderosa pine, the twisted juniper, and a variety of deciduous trees provide cool, shady places to picnic, relax and talk, strum guitars, or just laze the time away. Acres of grass, verdant and usually well watered, provide open space for the energetic to toss footballs or fling frisbees and whiz rings.

Fall brings out the high school and college cross-country team for workouts and occasional inter-school races. Joggers circle Drake Park all times of the year. Following a snowfall of three or more inches, the park offers nordic skiing possibilities within two blocks of the heart of Bend. Even night skiing is possible with illumination from nearby street lights.

The wildlife population of Mirror Pond includes Canada geese, mallard, pintail, widgeon, canvasback, ring-necked, and the red-head species of ducks. Swans are to be seen in Mirror Pond although they have a more permanent residence in Pioneer Park, or in secluded stretches of the Deschutes. Various other birds seen in Mirror Pond include the osprey, blue heron, coot, and falcon. The "City of Bend" budgets $600 to feed the water fowl in the winter when ice and snow create feeding problems. Feeding the ducks is a year-round activity for many Drake Park visitors.

Children often use the banks of the Deschutes to fish for trout or catch "crawdads." While the fishing is certainly far from the best in Central Oregon, the location of Drake Park and the Deschutes encourages much foot traffic to the fishing spots.

Harmon Park

Across the Deschutes River from Drake Park is a small, grassy play area which, if neglected by tourists, get considerable attention from Bend's youngsters. A playground with a nautical theme includes a small, snappy tug, the S.S. Happy Harmon, and a slide disguised as a lighthouse, along with more conventional play equipment. Adjacent to the children's play area, an open recreation field gets year-round use from schools by day, and in the summer evening it is the scene of some lively adult softball games.

Although Harmon Field is an attractive park today, the story of its creation reveals how difficult it often is to complete all the

The Deschutes River—looking across to Drake Park and upstream from the lawn of a residence of Pinelyn Park, platted 60 years ago. Overturf Butte is in background.

Drake Park is the final home for big wheels that were once used by loggers in the Deschutes country. The wheels are appropriately set against a background of Ponderosa pine.

An overall view of the beauty of the Deschutes River, Bend, taken a short distance downstream from the Mirror Pond parking lot. Cascade peaks provide a scenic background setting to help frame the river view. (Oregon State Highway photo)

Harmon Field is a popular park for impromptu games and organized recreation. It was developed, in part, through a grant from William E. Harmon, an eastern resident who never visited Bend.

steps from land acquisition to park dedication. Part of the story behind the park's development was reported in a June, 1953, issue of the Bend newspaper, telling how Harmon Field got its name:

It was named for a man who never saw Bend, the late William E. Harmon, eastern capitalist of early years. Deeply impressed by a 1,000-year-old playground for children in London, England, he returned to America and organized the Harmon Foundation for New York. Its purpose was to create playgrounds for children throughout the United States.

Residents of Bend heard of the objectives of the foundation, and through the Bend Kiwanis Club and under the leadership of the late J.A. Eastes, a bid for funds was made. Out of 150 applicants, Bend was selected for a grant.

Using the $2000 grant, the Kiwanis obtained land bordering the river, in the Harmon playfield area of the present. Through the years, with city, school and PWA cooperation, the field was extensively improved and two years ago was fenced. It is now considered one of the finest civic playgrounds in the state.[62]

This newspaper story, however, does not mention that the Harmon grant was made in 1924. Several thousands of dollars were spent in bringing in soil to the low-lying tract where, early in the twentieth century, "Marsh" Awbrey abandoned the land as a rye field. For years, the dust on the Harmon playground area became infamous as a "Dust Bowl." Several developments occurred up to 1939: some trees were planted, a wading pool was constructed, a playground building was erected, and even a monument was dedicated.

In the 1940's, a swimming pool was planned for the north end of the field. However, protest from nearby residents that property values would decline, commercialization would take over the area, and the peace and quiet of the neighborhood would be destroyed, helped stop that project. Bend finally found the site for its long-proposed outdoor pool—on the east side of town in Juniper Park.

Juniper Park

Largely through the efforts of former Bend mayor, Hans Slagsvold, Juniper Park was created out of 22 acres of wooded area on land acquired from Deschutes County for a mere $2000, in 1947. The name of the park, intended to emphasize the quality of trees in the area, was selected in August, 1952. Although Juniper Park is now surrounded by residential and commercial development, when the land was secured as a park, it was located in a remote, unsettled east part of town.

However, the site was a "natural" for a park, with little underbrush, big pines mixed in with countless junipers and numerous lava-rock outcrops. In 1949, after five years of planning and searching for an outdoor swimming-pool location, Juniper Park was selected as the site. That decision led to landscaping improvements in the park. Home builders, recognizing the aesthetics and convenience of a park location, quickly moved to the area.

During the next twenty years, various improvements and additions were made. A baseball field, designed for use by juveniles, was started early in 1953. Work on a concrete slab to be used for ice skating in winter and basketball at other times, was undertaken by Rotary Club members in August, 1962. At that time, plans were made for handball and tennis courts and an outdoor theater.

Fort Juniper, and adjacent Indian Village—a unique recreational attraction for youngsters—was constructed in the mid 1960's. Playground equipment was installed in December, 1964, with the help of the Jaycees. More recently, tennis courts have been added, and further acres of undeveloped land have been landscaped in Juniper Park.

Today, the park is the most diversified of all Bend's parks. Mothers supervise their youngsters clambering over the play equipment, teenagers toss basketballs, and older people converge on horseshoe courts. Swimming, tennis, and baseball are among the seasonal activities enjoyed here by Bend residents.

Fort Juniper, where cowboys and Indians can play in harmony, is but one part of Juniper Park. Elsewhere, in this eastside park, are tennis courts, baseball field, children's play equipment, and outdoor pool. Pilot Butte is in background.

Pioneer Park, small but attractive, is but one of 10 parks or park sites in Bend that are adjacent to the Deschutes River.

Pioneer Park

One of the smallest, but perhaps the most attractive, of Bend's parks, and certainly one of the popular visiting spots during the summertime is Pioneer Park. It is located along the east banks of the Deschutes River, a few blocks north of downtown Bend.

The name of the park stems from the belief that some early pioneers, the Clark party, crossed the Deschutes River at that place on their journey through Central Oregon in 1851. This belief, however, was refuted by Lindsy Sisemore, who questioned that the wagon trains would pick the steep rock-faced edge of the Deschutes to cross, when just upstream there is an excellent ford halfway between the Sisemore Place and the Staats Place in the vicinity of the mill pond.[63]

The city of Bend was given vacant property by Mrs. Carl H. Erickson. During the 1920's, the Pioneer Park location was the site of a city-owned auto campground. Travelers through Bend could make a campfire and pitch their tent in dust for a modest fee. The transition to the status of a city park occurred in 1928. Today, the verdant lawns in Pioneer Park are well watered during the dry summer by Bend District Parks and Recreation crews. Picnic tables dot the lawns, and during noontime in summer these tables are in almost constant use by visitors. The shady, tree-lined road into the park is often filled by autos, campers, and motor homes.

Several natural and man-made features contribute to Pioneer Park's beauty. A memorial rose garden, with dedication in memory of World War II, and an adjacent flower garden established by the Bend Garden Club, form the northern boundary of the park. At the height of summer, these gardens are a blaze of color. Rock walls, constructed in 1941, neatly and attractively mark the edge of Pioneer Park along the Deschutes. A short distance to the north, basaltic cliffs add another dimension to the landscape.

These weathered rimrocks, lined at the base with aspen and willow trees and shaded at the top by tall pines, help create an area of seclusion just 100 yards away from the busy park roadway. Along the rimrock base, a narrow pathway parallels the swift-flowing Deschutes but terminates at the Bend Riverside Condominiums, a short distance downstream. White-trunked aspens, their trunks carved with initials, and large lava rocks combine to further seclude those who stroll the banks of the Deschutes.

The river, swirling and turbulent as it flows past Pioneer Park, is steadied by a diversion dam, part of a 1920 Tumalo irrigation project, just downstream. Across the Deschutes, the lawns and the neatly manicured gardens of west-bank homes slope in picturesque fashion down to the river. Mature willows indicate that these homes have been established for many years. Swans fly, or swim back and forth, across the Deschutes, alternately seeking favors from park visitors and residents across the stream.

Pioneer Park's intensive use is short-lived. By mid-fall, leaves on the ash, maple and black locust trees—planted by man long ago—turn yellow and golden, then are quickly whisked to the lawns, whose deep green pales with the oncoming cold. As winter draws near, coupled with the end of the summer tourist season, Pioneer Park becomes a quiet, almost neglected part of Bend's landscape. Winter's snows are marked by few footprints and tire tracks, but as the seasons rotate and the cultural scene ebbs and flows, the waters from the Cascades continue their course past Pioneer Park, on their way to the Pacific Ocean.

Shevlin Park

The largest of Bend's parks is 380 acres of woodland, largely left in its natural state. Shevlin Park, located about four miles west of the city, has had an interesting history. Long ago, melt water from Cascade glaciers deposited a legacy of smooth cobbles in the Tumalo Creek stream bed and adjacent canyon floor. Lava flows have contributed large basaltic boulders, which are scattered throughout the canyon. White walls of volcanic ash flows, deposited by fiery avalanches, add further geological diversity to the Shevlin Park landscape.

Indians traversed the park's canyon floor long before the Fremont Party discovered and described the natural beauty of the area, on December 4, 1843. After following an Indian trail that ran south between the Deschutes River and the Cascades, Fremont's party camped on Tumalo Creek. Fremont's journal for that date read:

Shortly after we had left this encampment, the mountain trail from The Dalles joined that on which we were travelling. After passing for several miles over an artemisia plain, the trail entered a beautiful pine forest through which we travelled for several hours; and about 4 o'clock descended into the valley of another large branch, on the bottom of which were spaces of open pines, with occasional meadows of good grass, in one of which we camped. The stream is very swift and deep, and about 40 feet wide, and nearly half frozen over. Among the timber here, are larches 140 feet high, and over 3 feet in diameter. We had to-night the rare sight of a lunar rainbow.[64]

The Williamson railroad survey party used the same Indian trail that Fremont had taken and encamped at Tumalo Creek, September 3, 1855. The scenic qualities of Tumalo Creek, the small meadows and forested canyon slopes, were noted about 65 years later. In May, 1919, when logging was rapidly changing the forest landscapes in the Bend country, a plan to create a park along Tumalo Creek was made. *The Bulletin*, commenting on the plan, noted:

Nature has made the spot beautiful with pine trees, the pines that have made Bend what it is today. It is convenient to town for some purposes, it lies near the road to Broken Top (at that time, in 1919, the road to Broken Top from Bend passed along to the top of the west side of Tumalo Canyon) and in connection with the first hatchery, it can be developed into a real asset to the city.[65]

In November, 1919, the Shevlin-Hixon Company of Bend donated and dedicated, as a memorial to the late Thomas L. Shevlin, first president of the company, many acres of forested canyon along Tumalo Creek, with the condition that the company could cross the land with its logging railroad. The following month, the Bend Company, which had title to 150 acres along the canyon floor and along the bench above the canyon, donated its land to complete the park. These benevolent acts were recognized by the local newspaper. In an editorial, *The Bulletin* stated:

All who have visited the canyon recognize it as the most beautiful spot that there is within easy distance of town and will agree that its preservation for the enjoyment of the public is a service of the highest possible character.

In the flats adjoining the creek on the lower section of the proposed park grow quantities of shrubs, grasses and flowers not found in the arid lands above. Fir trees are found among the pine, and there are stands of larch, poplar and other deciduous trees.

As an example of what the canyon would be turned into in case it was not preserved as a park, there can be seen a 40-acre tract below the Orewilder mill site. This area was cut over last summer and it now lies bare and brown to the sky, offering a vivid comparison with the adjoining timbered canyon floor.

When President F.P. Hixon, of the Shevlin-Hixon Company, suggested a few weeks ago the possible creation of the Shevlin Memorial Park, Messrs. Baird and Orewilder were about to begin cutting in the canyon adjoining this 40-acre tract. Advised of the plan they readily consented to move to another location and the rest of the canyon was saved.[66]

Thus it is that residents of Bend, rather than witnessing the scalping of a unique scenic canyon just a few miles from town, inherited a "priceless possession."

In 1929, after negotiations with the Shevlin-Hixon Company, the city acquired the Tumalo Fish Hatchery and associated buildings for $300. The Oregon State Game Commission had previously abandoned the site because Tumalo Creek freezes during extremely cold weather. During the frigid winter of 1930, the Skyliners constructed a 225' x 125' ice-skating rink at the hatchery. Recently, the Bend Parks and Recreation District has restored ice skating to the old hatchery site.

The preservation of the park has not been without a fight. In the 1940's, the area adjacent to the park was logged, and the park itself was neglected.

A proposed plan, in 1950, called for construction of a dam on Tumalo Creek, downstream from the park, which if it had materialized, would have provided winter water storage for the Tumalo Project, but at the same time would have flooded part of the park. Although the dam was not completed, the industrious work of beavers resulted in beaver dams that flooded part of both the upper and lower meadows before the Oregon Game Commission transferred the beavers. The infamous December, 1964, rainstorm scattered boulders, rocks and debris along the banks of Tumalo Creek, and undermined the road through the park. The following year, two proposals were made to build a dam, either 50 feet or 150 feet in height, to regulate the flow of Tumalo Creek. If built at the latter height, the upper meadow would have been flooded.

In recent years, other plans would have modified parts of the Shevlin Park landscape. Attempts to prepare the disused Brooks-Scanlon railroad bed for a bike-hiking trail, connecting either Bend or the old Skyliner Road with Shevlin Park, were discussed on several occasions after being brought up in December, 1966. In 1971, a proposal to build a 275-seat amphitheater adjacent to the main park road was shelved, following protests by environmentally conscious citizens who felt that Shevlin Park should be kept natural.

As a Bicentennial project, the 40' x 80' building that long ago served as a State Fish Hatchery was renovated and restored to its original rustic style, then converted into a community and recreational center. The project, envisioned and led by Vince

Genna, Bend Parks and Recreation District Director, was completed through community spirit—with Brooks-Scanlon Company making major contributions of wood products, and with labor donated by park board members, park department employees and other Bend citizens. Additional labor was provided by a movie construction crew, in exchange for use of Shevlin Park as a setting for part of the filming of *Rooster Cogburn.*

Shevlin Park has long been a popular picnic place for families and organizations. The park's attenuated shape, stretched out along the canyon of Tumalo Creek, helps disperse users of the park, except at the lower and upper meadows where the confined rough grassy areas provide open areas for softball games. Between the meadows, lush vegetation, sliced by a fast-flowing stream, attracts birds and deer to the woodland.

The park serves many different people. In summer, organized groups use Shevlin Park for nature studies. Children frequent the park for fishing Tumalo Creek. High school and college cross-country teams have ready-made courses with trails winding along shaded trails, across rustic bridges and up challenging canyon slopes.

Shevlin Park offers an excellent destination for bicycle riders, and the three-mile paved road through the forest is easy riding. Those who seek solitude, scenery and relaxation—a mere few minutes' drive from urban Bend—often stroll through Shevlin Park, especially in the fall and winter. During the fall, the soft, yellow needles of the tamarack add subtle coloring to the reds, oranges, and evergreens, all mixed together in close proximity. Winter snows contribute another dimension to the Shevlin Park landscapes.

After more than half a century as a Bend city park, Shevlin Park has managed to maintain its natural look.

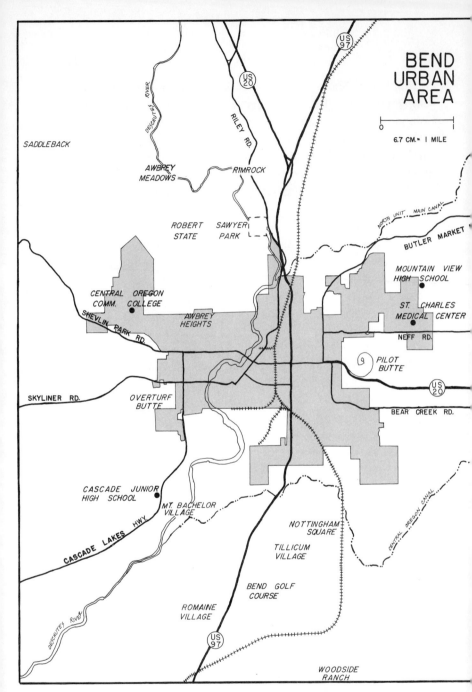

The Bend urban area has a population of about 30,000 and is growing at a rapid rate. Many people prefer living in rural subdivisions, or on acreages. It is estimated by planners that 45,000 will live in the Bend area by 1985. Map shows location of rural subdivisions and other major landmarks in the area. Overlay shows city boundary.

6.

BEND—THE LIVABLE CITY

We have noted the natural landscapes of Bend, the growth of the city, and the major landmarks. In this section, we shall discuss Bend as a "livable city" and Bend in its regional setting. Some of its unique aesthetic landscapes and its surrounding residential area are noted by Ned Langford in Volume III of the Bend Urban Area Plan:

> The irregular terrain and the natural vegetation of juniper and sage or pine give the area a distinctive visual quality. . . . The combination of irregular terrain and natural vegetation limit views and vistas within the community so that the general impression is that the community is smaller and less spread out than it actually is. . . . The appearance, quality of development, natural setting, climate, and values have served to make Bend one of the more desirable places in Oregon to live.[67]

Newcomers to Bend have the choice of several different residential areas, some long established, some new, some with modest homes, some with spacious homes. Two subdivisions which have a "Country Club" landscape appearance are Woodside Ranch and Saddleback, each located a few miles from Bend. Large homesites, averaging 2-1/2 acres have been developed in a natural setting which includes pine, juniper, clumps of bright green manzanita, lava outcrops, and the ever desirable views of the Cascades. Attractive custom-built homes, using the natural look of wood for siding and shake roofs, help blend the structures into the natural environement. With utilities placed underground, large lots, and planned use of the natural environments, these suburban developments have a rural-type landscape—yet they are within a few miles of downtown Bend.

North of town, adjacent to the Deschutes River, homesites in the Rimrock Subdivision are scenically placed on the rimrocks overlooking the river or, in places, are nestled between the rimrock walls and the rock-strewn stream bed.

Elsewhere in the Bend urban area, planned communities include Tillicum Village, Nottingham Square, and Timber Ridge. The concept of cluster neighborhoods set in a park-like landscape with common open spaces, and homesites secluded by juniper and pine, contributes to the pleasant aesthetic appearance of these subdivisions. Most of the houses are ranch style, using shake roofs and natural colors in the siding. Romaine Village is an attractively designed community for mobile homes, set in the midst of a pine forest. It features its own recreational center, including a clubhouse, an indoor heated swimming pool, and exercise room.

Residential dwellers located in the "flat" and more arid lands east of Bend have to work with scattered juniper and sage. In places, outcrops of lava rocks and "faults" either obscure homes or provide elevated sites with panoramic vistas of the Cascades—which often extend from Mt. Hood in the north to Bachelor Butte. In this rural part of Bend, modest homes and spacious ranch homes dot the prairie-like landscape.

Within the city itself, new and older established residential areas are scattered throughout the city. Fashionable homes tend to dominate the neighborhoods adjacent to Drake Park and Mirror Pond, also those in the West Hills, Eastwood, and scattered peripheral rural sections. Each neighborhood has its own personality. For example, homes in the Drake Park area are, for the most part, large two-story mansions, each with a

This pastoral scene northwest of Bend focuses on the role of man in bringing water to cleared juniper forests. Three Fingered Jack, Black Butte and Mt. Jefferson are in background (left to right). (Bill Van Allen photo)

Donna Gill's Rock Springs Ranch, 6 miles northwest of Bend, offers guests tennis, swimming, horseback riding, and western hospitality in a scenic setting. Separate cottages overlook green meadows. A lodge serves as the focal point for meals and conversation.

unique charm and character. Their location, adjacent to Mirror Pond and the tranquil Deschutes River, is one of the most prestigious in Bend. Elsewhere, residential neighborhoods include a mixture of neat ranch-style homes constructed in recent years, or older small frame homes built following the completion of the railroad in 1911, or the large lumber mills in 1916.

Undoubtedly an important part of the residential landscape scenes in Bend is the heterogeneous nature of social-economic neighborhoods, all in relative close proximity to one another but each characterized by unique natural or cultural features. Older homes on dusty, unpaved roads are very much a visible part of the urban scene in Bend. Here, college students, full-time ski enthusiasts, and "others" who find Bend a livable town have their "pads."

While some of the older homes in Bend have a rather dilapidated appearance, many houses of similar vintage have been well cared for. It is not difficult to discover freshly painted houses picturesquely set amidst attractive yards. Collectively, all of the neighborhoods contribute to a diversity of residential landscapes, which is quite remarkable for a small city.

In addition to Bend's physical and cultural diversity and its desirable sunny climate, part of the city's appeal is its geographical location—its proximity to mountains, forests, lakes, canyon-land, deserts, and youthful volcanic activity.

Residents and visitors to the city are able to select from a variety of year-round recreational opportunities. Some of these recreational areas are but a few miles out of town; others, like Crater Lake National Park or Kah-Nee-Tah, the plush Warm Springs Indian resort, are little more than 1-1/2 hours' drive.

In recent years, Bend's popularity as a center for winter sports has grown considerably. Alpine and Nordic skiing were introduced to the area by Scandinavian migrants who, via Minnesota, brought their lumbering and skiing skills to Bend. However, Bend's growth in alpine skiing has occurred only since Bachelor Butte became accessible. Then it developed as a ski resort in the 1960's and 1970's. Mt. Bachelor Ski Resort, which

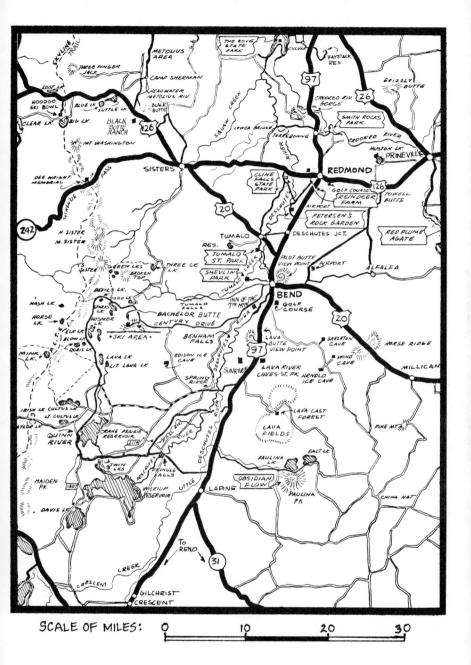

SCALE OF MILES: 0   10   20   30

Scenic attractions in Central Oregon. Bend is a focal point for visiting numerous lakes, lava caves, Mt. Bachelor Ski Area, wilderness areas in the Cascades, and east of Bend, the High Desert.

West of Bend is Broken Top, an old, deeply eroded volcano. (Joe Van Wormer photo)

now boasts seven chairlifts and usually at least six months of skiing—often with deep powdery snow—lies but twenty miles from Bend. Bend residents who are fortunate enough to adjust their weekday work schedule can leave town at noon, get in seven or eight runs, and be home for five o'clock dinner.

Nordic skiers, and there are increasingly more of them in Bend, can select from a wide range of scenic winter trails which are geared to beginner, intermediate and expert skiers. Within a fifteen minutes' drive of Bend, cross-country skiers can arrive at trailheads and trek through fragrant pine forests to snow-covered Swampy Lakes, or to secluded Tumalo Falls. A few miles farther from Bend, Dutchman Flat, near Bachelor Butte, is a departure point for ski trips to scenic Todd Lake or Sparks Lake. The solitude and quiet winter beauty of the Three Sisters Wilderness Area can easily be reached by intermediate nordic skiers.

Ice-skating enthusiasts can enjoy their sport at the Sunriver or Inn of the Seventh Mountain resorts, both a few miles from Bend. With a prolonged cold spell, the Bend Parks and Recreation District is able to provide ice skating in town at Juniper Park, or at the renovated Shevlin Park Fish Hatchery, three miles from Bend. Areas designated for snowmobiling have been established along the road to Mt. Bachelor Ski Resort, at Newberry Crater, and along the McKenzie Pass highway. Certainly, for many residents, part of the livability of Bend is participation in winter sports.

Each spring melting snow and access to the high country of the Cascades opens up a score of lakes and hundreds of miles of hiking trails. These trails, in turn, lead to colorful alpine meadows, and close-up vistas of glacier-clad peaks and jagged lava flows. Such is the location of Bend that, within an hour's travel, the hustle and bustle of a growing urban area can be left behind and replaced by pine-scented mountain air, the rush of tumbling streams like Tumalo Creek or Fall Creek, or by the tranquility to be found at Elk Lake, Sparks Lake, or in the Three Sisters Wilderness Area.

Closer to Bend, along the Deschutes River, are numerous picturesque spots that beckon the fisherman, canoeist, sightseer or picnicker. In places, the Deschutes has cut through mounds of black lava rock which spilled from Lava Butte some 6,000 years ago. Here, the river cascades turbulent white water through the constricted channels. Yet, just a few yards distant, the Deschutes River settles down and meanders through grassy meadows that are bordered by tall Ponderosa pines.

"Recent" volcanism, with youthful-looking cinder cones, vast lava and obsidian flows, ice caves, and other volcanic features, virtually border the southern rural areas of Bend. Elsewhere, within twenty-five miles of Bend, are numerous other examples of volcanic features, some readily identified by the lay person; others discernible to the amateur and professional geologist. Volcanic areas are often noted for their stark beauty and spectacular scenery. Central Oregon residents can discover such landscapes in their own "backyards."

A few miles to the east of Bend is yet another landscape type—the desert lands of Central Oregon, where homesteaders vainly attempted to wrestle a living from the sand and sagebrush. These vast, arid lands consist of remnants of ancient lakes, abrupt rimrocks, scattered juniper trees and lonely homesteads. The countryside to the north of Bend is predominantly characterized by juniper lands and grasslands. In places, deep canyons provide spectacular vistas where rivers have incised into thick, ancient lava flows. Hydroelectric dams on the Deschutes River have created large bodies of water sheltered by towering rimrocks. Here there are boating activities and lakeshore camp sites.

Many Central Oregonians enjoy the recreation of rockhounding, and the hobby of polishing rocks. Popular areas for rockhounds include the forested Ochocos, the more isolated Maury Mountains, and scattered locations in the grasslands northeast of Madras. Annual powwows held at Prineville and Madras each July attract rockhounders from all over the United States.

While a diversity of residential areas, nearby recreational opportunities, and a beautiful setting all contribute to the

Bachelor Butte (9060 feet)—whose northern slopes support 7 chairlifts—has rapidly become a major ski resort in the Pacific Northwest with extensive runs on dry powder snow. Dutchman Flat (left foreground) is a popular ski touring area. Note line of cinder cones behind Bachelor Butte. White areas in background are frozen lakes. (Don Peters, Bend, photo)

Alpine skiers descending the northern slopes of Bachelor Butte have distracting views of nearby peaks of the Cascades. Mountains in background include (left to right) South Sister, Middle Sister, North Sister, and Broken Top. (Oregon State Highway photo)

Aerial view of Newberry Volcano looking south. East Lake (left) and Paulina Lake (right) are favorites for anglers. Obsidian flow (background) can be reached by paved road inside the caldera. Newberry Volcano is about one hour's drive south of Bend. (Oregon State Game Commission photo)

Forest sliced by Cascades Lakes Highway (left). Lakes visible in this aerial view are Elk and Hosmer (background), with Lava and Little Lava lakes in foreground. Deschutes River flows out of Little Lava Lake. (USFS photo)

livability of the community, other less tangible criteria are also important. Good medical and educational facilities are readily available. And strong citizen interest in the town, its schools, and planning processes indicate a bright future for Bend.

The size of the town is, for many people, an ideal one, with enough people to have a variety of services and retail outlets without journeying across the Cascades to Portland. Yet the near 30,000 urban population is not so large that the political structure of the city and the county are burdensome or out of hand.

Yet, as these thoughts are put into writing, the population growth rate for the urban area is accelerating and land-use changes are occurring almost overnight. The popularity of desirable places becomes contagious and, in the case of Bend, the attractions of the area are such that the character of the city and adjacent urban and rural lands is being modified at a rapid rate.

Bend now stands at the threshold of another surge of population increase. We have already seen that irrigation waters in the early 1900's, the coming of the railroad in 1911, the establishment of two giant lumber mills in 1916, and the growth of tourism and recreation after World War II, have been key economic landmarks which have significantly encouraged Bend's growth at different intervals. Economic indicators at this time point to even more dramatic increases in population because of large construction projects already planned. Resulting changes in the landscape of the urban area are inevitable. It is now evident that Bend can no longer be called that "quaint small mill town east of the Cascades."

Planners project that the Bend urban area will contain 45,000 people by 1985. Beyond that date, population projections and landscape appearances become increasingly speculative. In 1960, *The Bulletin* featured an article which focused on planning in Bend, including a look ahead to 1980. Following is the paper's perception of Bend for 1980:

Left: The Deschutes River south of Bend flows through miles of pine trees within the Deschutes National Forest. The river, accessible at many places, periodically changes its moods, as it cuts through lava flows or meanders across meadows. (Oregon State Highway photo)

Right: North of Bend, in Jefferson County, west of Madras, the landscapes are characterized by extensive plateaus incised by rivers. Here, near Lake Billy Chinook, the Deschutes River and the Crooked River (foreground) are separated by a narrow peninsula (called "The Island"). This part of Central Oregon is noted for water recreation, camping and scenic geology. In the background is Mt. Jefferson.

Tumalo Reservoir, located about 10 miles northwest of Bend, provides quiet waters for canoeing, and a mirror-like reflection of Three Sisters for photographers. (Don Peters photo)

An "educated guess" at the future Bend might have it looking like this:

Downtown, there are shiny, modern store fronts. No parking is allowed downtown, because the parking lanes are needed for the heavy traffic. Around the fringes of the core area are metered parking lots, within walking distance of downtown shops. Greenwood Avenue, N. First and possibly S. Third, are lined with motels, restaurants, and other tourist facilities. Highway 97 has been moved out to the other side of Pilot Butte. Pilot Butte itself is an island in a sea of houses. The small development-type bungalows have moved eastward almost as far as the 97 freeway.

Upstream, along the Deschutes, we find heavy industry. Beyond the Brooks-Scanlon lumber mill is a pulp and paper mill. On the other side, on the site of the old Shevlin-Hixon mill, is an industrial park, housing two or three medium-heavy industries.

There are few parks that didn't exist in 1960. But the riverside parks have been extended, and the east bank of the river is now one solid city park from the south city limits to Pioneer Park. The other bank also has large stretches of green.

All principal streets are now four lanes. A new street, called a "perimeter street," to run all around the city, is being constructed. This street, when completed, will allow quicker driving from one side of town to the other.

Visionary? Perhaps. But most of the above items have been predicted by one city official or another. And if the planning keeps pace with the growth, it is a prospect we will have no cause to fear.[68]

To discuss the landscapes of Bend for the year 2000 is extremely speculative. Growth is seemingly inevitable, though there are strong forces in Bend to contain such growth. There are still those who have a nostalgia for Bend as it was before 1960. Equally strong, and perhaps more forceful, are thrusts to encourage growth.

The important element in planning for the Bend urban area is control of this growth. All concerned citizens must actively participate in the planning process to ensure that, as far as possible, the landscapes of the city continue to show the character, image and livability which we hope this book has portrayed.[69]

NOTES

1. *Bend Bulletin*, September 18, 1903.
2. Koji Mimura, *The Geological Society of America*, Vol. 10, No. 3, February, 1978.
3. *Deschutes Echo*, January 17, 1903.
4. Kathy Bowman, unpublished manuscript, 1976.
5. *Bend Bulletin*, September 13, 1947.
6. W.D. Cheney, *Central Oregon* (1918), p. 91.
7. *Bend Bulletin*, July 10, 1903.
8. Raymond R. Hatton, *Bend Country Weather and Climate* (1977).
9. Lewis L. McArthur, *Oregon Geographic Names* (1974), p. 40.
10. *Bend Bulletin*, June 28, 1911.
11. *Deschutes Echo*, January 17, 1903.
12. *Bend Bulletin*, May 4, 1910.
13. *Deschutes Echo*, December 20, 1902.
14. Urling Coe, *Frontier Doctor* (1940), pp. 2-4.
15. *Ibid.*, p. 4.
16. *Bend Bulletin*, April 20, 1906.
17. *Ibid.*, April 21, 1905.
18. W.D. Cheney, *The Bend Book* (1911), p. 7.
19. *Ibid.*, pp. 34-35.
20. *Bend Bulletin*, December 15, 1909.
21. *Ibid.*, January 12, 1910.
22. *Ibid.*, May 4, 1910.
23. *Ibid.*
24. *Ibid.*, January 23, 1910.
25. *Ibid.*, July 30, 1912.
26. *Ibid.*, August 30, 1911.
27. *Ibid.*, April 10, 1912.
28. *Ibid.*, July 3, 1912.
29. *Ibid.*, December 4, 1912.
30. *Ibid.*, July 9, 1913.
31. *Ibid.*, July 2, 1913.
32. *Ibid.*, April 28, 1915.
33. *Deschutes Pioneers Gazette*, January, 1976.
34. *Ibid.*, January, 1974.
35. Pamela West, "The Rise and Fall of the American Porch," *Landscape*, Vol. 20, No. 3, Spring, 1976.
36. *Bend Bulletin*, November 4, 1921.
37. *Bend Bulletin*, July 3, 1912.
38. *Ibid.*
39. *Ibid.*, August 4, 1919.
40. *Ibid.*, August 3, 1920.
41. *Ibid.*, August 26, 1921.
42. *Ibid.*, August 29, 1928.
43. *Ibid.*, May 19, 1936.

44. *Ibid.*, October 13, 1919.
45. Keith Clark and Lowell Tiller, *Terrible Trail: The Meek Cut-Off, 1845* (1966), pp. 101-102.
46. *Ibid.*, p. 113.
47. Israel, Russell, *Geology and Water Resources of Central Oregon* (1905), p. 95.
48. ＿＿ Cheney, pp. 88-89; 115-116.
49. *Bend Bulletin*, April 29, 1914.
50. *Oregon Historical Quarterly*, Vol. #29, (December, 1928), p. 364.
51. *The Bulletin*, April 14, 1965.
52. *Ibid.*, June 7, 1928.
53. *Ibid.*, June 8, 1957.
54. Conversation with Bill Smith, president, Brooks Resources, Bend, May 1, 1977.
55. *The Bulletin*, June 14, 1963.
56. *Ibid.*, August 29, 1963.
57. *Bend Bulletin*, April 3, 1903.
58. *Ibid.*, April 21, 1916.
59. *Ibid.*, June 8, 1933.
60. *Ibid.*, July 5, 1939.
61. *Ibid.*, July 5, 1960.
62. *Ibid.*, June 16, 1953.
63. *Ibid.*, August 3, 1940.
64. Reprint in *The Bulletin*, August 13, 1942, with an editorial by Robert W. Sawyer suggesting that the upper meadow be given the name Fremont Meadow.
65. *Bend Bulletin*, May 8, 1919.
66. *Ibid.*, December 3, 1919.
67. Philip C. Patterson, Ned M. Langford, and Lyle A. Stewart, *Bend Area General Plan* from Parts I and III (1974).
68. *Bend Bulletin*, August 24, 1960.
69. See the *Bend Area General Plan* prepared by Patterson, Langford and Stewart (Medford) which discusses goals, objectives, and recommendations for planning.

BIBLIOGRAPHY

Appleton, Jay. *The Experience of Landscape*. London: John Wiley and Sons, 1975.

Baldwin, Ewart M. *Geology of Oregon*. Ann Arbor, Michigan: Edwards Bros., 1964.

Brodatz, Phil and Dori Watson. *The Elements of Landscape*. New York: Reinhold Book Corp., 1968.

Brogan, Phil F. *East of the Cascades*. Portland: Binfords & Mort, Publishers, 1964.

Bulletin, The (Bend), 1903-1976. (Formerly *The Bend Bulletin*)

Cheney, W.D. *The Bend Book*. 1911.

_____ . *Central Oregon*. Portland: The Ivy Press, 1918.

Clark, Keith and Lowell Tiller. *Terrible Trail: The Meek Cut-Off, 1845*. Caldwell, Idaho: The Caxton Printers, Ltd., 1966.

Coe, Urling C. *Frontier Doctor*. New York: Macmillan Publishing Co., 1940.

Crowell, James L. *Frontier Publisher: George Palmer Putnam*. MA Thesis, University of Oregon, 1966.

Dicken, Samuel. *Geography of Oregon*. Ann Arbor, Michigan: Edwards Bros., 1965.

Eaton, Walter P. *Skyline Camps*. Boston, Chicago: W.A. Wilde, Publishers, 1922.

Erickson, Sheldon D. *Occupance in the Upper Deschutes Basin, Oregon*. Research Paper No. 32. Chicago, Illinois: The University of Chicago, 1953.

Hatton, Raymond. *Bend Country Weather and Climate*. Redmond: Mid-State Printing, 1977.

Jones, Stuart E. "Oregon's Many Faces," *National Geographic*. Vol. 135, No. 1, January, 1969.

Lucia, Ellis. *Klondike Kate*. New York: Ballantine Books, 1962.

Mimura, Koji. *The Geological Society of America*. Vol. 10, No. 3, February, 1978.

Patterson, Philip C., Ned M. Langford, and Lyle A. Stewart. *Bend Area General Plan*. Medford, Oregon, 1975.

Peterson, Norman V., Edward A. Groh, Edward M. Taylor, Donald F. Stensland. *Geology and Mineral Resources of Deschutes County, Oregon*. Portland: State of Oregon Department of Geology and Mineral Resources, 1976.

Putnam, George Palmer. *In the Oregon Country*. New York: The Knickerbocker Press, 1915.

_____ . *The Smiting of the Rock*. New York: Grossett and Dunlap, 1918.

Tuan, Yi-Fu. *Topophilia*. Englewood Cliffs, New Jersey: Prentice-Hall, 1974.

_____ . "Place: An Experiential Perspective," *The Geographical Review*. Vol. 65, No. 2. April, 1975.

West, Pamela. "The Rise and Fall of the American Porch," *Landscape*. Vol. 20, No. 3, Spring, 1976.

Williams, Howell. *A Geological Map of the Bend Quadrangle, Oregon*. State of Oregon Dept. of Geology and Mineral Industries, 1957.

INDEX

(Page numbers of photos and special map entries in black type)